TOWARD THE UNKNOWN

Memoirs of an American Fighter Pilot

By... Colonel Charles (Chuck) Maultsby USAF

Edited by: Charles Maultsby II

Copyright 2013 by Charles Maultsby II

All rights reserved.

Dedicated to the Real Heroes...

"My Friends who shared anguish and mirth,

Then slipped the surly bonds of earth."

Captain Charles D. "Fish" Salmon

Major Robert S. "Fitz" Fitzgerald

Major Rudolph Anderson, Jr.

Captain John R. "Dick" Crane

Captain Joe G. Hyde, Jr.

L to R: Dick Crane-Martin Caiden-Chuck Maultsby 1959

Author Martin Caidin (pictured center) flew with the Thunderbirds as an honorary member for six weeks while researching his book, *THUNDERBIRDS*. Martin wrote 50 books including *CYBORG*, first published in 1972, that was adopted for television as *The Six Million Dollar Man*. His novel *Marooned* was made in to a 1969 movie starring Gregory Peck, Richard Crenna, David Janssen and Gene Hackman.

CONTENTS

Foreword by Martin Caidin ... vi

Foreword by Colonel Chuck Maultsby ... x

Chapter 1   The Bad Boyhood ... 1

Chapter 2   The Budding Pilot ... 13

Chapter 3   Northrop and Family ... 39

Chapter 4   Pilot Training ... 54

Chapter 5   Okinawa 1951 ... 87

Chapter 6   Bailout/P.O.W. ... 103

Chapter 7   How to Become a Thunderbird ... 117

Chapter 8   The Cost of Glory ... 153

Chapter 9   U-2 and Me ... 165

Chapter 10 Vietnam ... 218

EPILOG ... 247

Afterword   By Chuck W. Maultsby II ... 253

Further Reading ... 255

Foreword by ...Martin Caidin

The odds against his ever becoming a pilot were staggering. Invariably it takes financing, or the ability to scab rides with pilots by washing planes or running errands, but Chuck Maultsby didn't quite have the moments to do so. When you begin life on an emotional roller coaster, and your family is sundered at the worst possible early age, just hanging on to reason and peering into a murky future is tough enough.

As Chuck Maultsby puts it succinctly: "There were more lows than highs." This manner of understatement would be his mark through his life and they revealed the steadfastness with which he would hammer at the dreadful odds against him. Memory recalls the highs as those years with his mother and four sisters, right through the worst of the depression years.

Family love was the bedrock that bore them through the worst, but even that shattered violently when his mother died, when he was wrenched from his sisters who were unlovingly packed off to a "school for girls," and Maultsby swung darkly into living with a father he found a man to be feared.

There must be a spark in every youngster's life that will remain lit, even though smoldering for years that will be waiting to be brought again to full fire.

The young boy was literally rescued from his father by an aunt and uncle who brooked no nonsense in taking the youth to live with them in Norfolk, Virginia.

The bleak memories settled deep within him from the affection and care he found so suddenly, and… well, the spark.

A special moment of his life occurred when he was five years old. He was taken to an open field where before him was, for a boy, a huge gleaming-silver winged giant! Monstrous wings, three thundering engines, the smell of oil and gasoline, the friendly grins of the pilots, and Chuck Maultsby tasted the miracle of flight as he stared awe stricken from the window of the Ford Tri-Motor that first bore him aloft.

That was a promise of tomorrow, and what he could not grasp for another decade to come, finally was within his reach by dint of a never-forgotten oath to himself that he would one day fly, he would become a pilot.

And he did. He scraped together the money for lessons. He scrounged and like so many other airport fence-hangers he built his dual time, and then came his 16th birthday. He sat alone in the back seat of a yellowed Piper J-3 Cub, the heels of his feet dancing back and forth on the rudder pedals. Straining to see over the long nose, the throttle moving forward under his left hand, right rudder to counter torque, the little engine crashing sound back at him, wind rising, and the tail came up and kept her down the runway. Then came the wonder that attends every flight was his and he soared into the sky.

There is an old and true saying among the legions of pilots. No matter who you are or what you have ever accomplished, no pilot ever gets more than one first solo! Chuck Maultsby had entered the ranks.

At first glance, hardly the most auspicious moment of flight for anyone save the kid gripping the stick in his right hand and the throttle knob in his left. But from such moments come the future that no one can foretell, and who would know that this same youth would one day be...

Hurtling up and over in a gigantic loop in a supersonic jet fighter, tucked in a throat gripping tight formation with three other Super Sabres, swinging aloft over the earth in that magnificent precision flying for which the world-famous Thunderbirds are known. In that diamond formation, flying right wing, was the same kid who'd felt the wind, the vibration, the thunder, and feel of the earth falling away beneath him in the corrugated *Tin Goose* as they called the ancient Ford.

There would be moments, adventures, disasters, challenges, and growth of skill to where Chuck Maultsby would be considered one of the finest and most skilled pilots from among the best in the world. He would know a moment in October of 1962 when his friend and neighbor, Major Rudolf Anderson, was being shot down over Cuba. ...And Maultsby?

High over the Soviet Union in a black spy plane, the famous U-2, penetrating deep into Russian airspace on his mission... which enraged President John F. Kennedy who, forgetting that Maultsby was an Air Force pilot flying for the Air Force, and his country, was following orders, and remarked in his anger that, "There is always some son of a bitch that doesn't get the word! What the hell is that man doing over Russia when we're trying to avoid a war?"

It's a hell of a high water mark for a man known only

inside the closed circle of pilots, but it pales against combat missions over Korea, being shot down, being beaten, tortured, and brainwashed by the Communist Chinese. And there is the harrowing story of two hundred and sixteen combat missions in the huge and powerful F-4C Phantom in Viet Nam.

But this gets ahead of a story that needs its telling in that same gripping understatement that's the mark of Chuck Maultsby. It's pure Americana all the way, apple pie and the flag, purple mountains majesty, dedication, and a belief in what he had to do for family, a nation's people and the country itself. It's as modern as a howling supersonic fighter and terrible bombing raids, and as old-fashioned as principals of patriotism, faith in himself and his country.

In what holds such great promise as a book to be treasured by those who love flying, by so many more who believe in and cherish their nation, this is the "phases" of his life as Maultsby describes them in his own words…

*   *   *

TOWARD THE UNKNOWN

Memoirs of an American Fighter Pilot

Foreword by... Colonel Chuck W. Maultsby USAF

I write these memoirs, these moments and events of life, love and wonder, of being savaged by fire and pain, of being blown out of the sky. Memoirs of being embroiled in the barbarism of a modern world most Americans had relegated to ancient history... but was the lot of so many of us.

I've been called a hero. I deny the call. Oh, there are heroes all right, and every one of them I ever knew is buried somewhere in a field no one remembers, or their bones have sunk to the deep bottom of a swallowing and uncaring sea. Men who only moments before were living flesh and blood, with smiles endearing them to their families. Intelligent men, bursting with promise, who in an instant were crisped by searing flames to a gut wrenching sight instead of what had been a wonderful, warm, human being and soul. There were other heroes we never saw again, consumed and obliterated in a single instant; that terrible flash when a fighter tears itself to pieces in the sky, or pulverizes itself and its hapless human occupant in a final sharp crack followed by the fading roll of thunder.

I really don't know much about heroes except for the men I saw withstand torture beyond description, men who were burning alive and kept flying their planes, men who were sworn to do their job for their country.

There it is. It's very old fashioned, even antique and perhaps out of style for so many of us. I'm talking about values, patriotism and a determination to protect and keep what our forefathers created out of a wilderness of meanness; a determination to protect our nation from mad leaders of powerful nations who so eagerly sought our destruction.

It was my job. MY job… and I did it the best I could. It was many things, including sweat and pain, laughter and sharing, exultation and bitterness, grief and loss of friends and loved ones.

Do you know who the other heroes were? They were the heroes who didn't wear uniforms. The wives were the heroes. Year after year, shifting from one home to another knowing their husbands were aloft in fighter planes that cost ten, twenty and even thirty million dollars who would come home to miserable rented rooms, trailers or shacks, who scrimped to feed the kids and pay the doctors. And no matter how bad it ever became, they greeted those pilots with love, warmth and above all, with understanding.

There are more dead men behind us than we'll ever know who failed to have the support of the women they loved. Start a fight with your fighter pilot husband and you've just increased the odds that either he'll come home as charred chunks in a GI-issue basket, or they'll drop a wreath from the sky over a dark smear against a mountainside where "he went in."

There's no room in a killing machine for second thoughts. Not unless you don't mind dying stupidly and senselessly.

But I was talking about heroes... those of us who struggled upward against the odds, who roared or stumbled into lethal combat day after day-night after night. Well, I never knew any of us who ever used that word "hero" because it didn't fit. Certainly, from our point of view, it didn't fit us. Ours was just a job. The kind of job that's kept America free. Yes, pick and shovel in the cockpit of a supersonic jet fighter.

Just a job? Soaring over the Soviet Union, or hunting down the secrets of bombers, missiles and millions of soldiers, while two nations trembled on the brink of nuclear war?

You don't think about that when you're so high that you can see the faint but unmistakable curvature of the earth in the distance. You think of what the dials tell you; your fuel pressure, airspeed, tailpipe temperature. You think about not stalling out in that horribly thin and naked air and you think about whether you'll ever get home again to see your wife and kids because you're at 70,000 feet up in the middle of nowhere... smack in the middle of the enemy camp.

Do you want to get home? Then do your job. I did... and my friends did. Not all of us came home... Damn it! We will always miss them and it doesn't matter that the country doesn't know their names. How could anyone know who these people were? You never saw them riding the sharp edge of a sword down into the abyss... but after all, that was our job.

It was my job, even if the president of my country nailed me to the press of the whole blamed world as that "son of a bitch that doesn't get the word." I have always wondered if the Russians at their missile batteries, if the Russian pilots climbing up to do their best to kill me... I've wondered if they laughed at my president's description of this man, me, defying their laws and penetrating their airspace.

If I had been a Russian I'd have laughed the whole week. William Saroyan would have laughed too. That's why he called our wars and our posturing *The Human Comedy*. Real funny. Grisly, I guess, but through the years we've laughed a lot about that.

There are all kinds of kids who have all kinds of lives. Some are better than others, some are worse than others, but no matter what they are, they're the patchwork quilt of youth that all youngsters share-even if from the wrong side of the tracks or some other lonely place where the fates have dealt the kids a hand from the bottom of the deck. I always figured, because this was reality, I was more at the bottom of the roller coaster rather than enjoying the view from the top; before the daring, giggling, shrieking plunge downward, yet always knowing you were coming up again.

I missed my sisters, all four of them. I missed when we would huddle together and try to understand the pain knifing through us because our mother was... what was the word... dead? Do you know what "dead" means to kids who are hurt, baffled and wounded? It means distancing themselves from the frightening and horrible adult world because it killed our mother. It got even worse when I went one way and the four girls I loved now more than anyone or anything else in the world was ripped away from our desperate togetherness.

But the sun always comes up even if many of the mornings were bleak and darker than they should have been. I was five years old when I first soared into the sky in that great, corrugated metal bird stinking so wonderfully of oil, gasoline and sweat. I didn't know it then, but that was the trigger striking home, smacking into the firing pin... but I wouldn't hear it inside my head until I was fifteen and doing anything to learn to fly.

I did learn to fly and soloed at sixteen, and oh God... it was marvelous! It was freedom ...sailing above the earth, laughing with the birds, feeling the wind gusts trembling the fabric-my body-the machine, knowing that when I sighed gently back to earth that I had found my niche. I was going to damn well become a pilot ...and a hell of a good pilot!

Do you know what was so wonderful then? I never had so much as the flimsiest dream that I would ever fly so high, far and fast with the best pilots in the world. There are the best of times and the worst of times for all of us, but for me there is nothing ever so special as the wonder of flight... to see the cloud mountains, the purple twilight, the punch of air and the squeeze of g-forces. I somehow tasted all of these wonders on that first solo flight on my sixteenth birthday. Then the years speeded up, and while in these pages of introduction the details must necessarily be left out, I was headed toward what I wanted so desperately to be... an aviation cadet, a military pilot... a fighter pilot by God!

So… When I turned eighteen years old I shined my shoes, put on a clean shirt, scrubbed my face, slicked down my hair and went off to enlist.

In those days it was still the Army Air Corps and I had the dubious distinction of being a Pre-Aviation Cadet. I wasn't flying, but instead I was studying books, cleaning the barracks, doing close order drill, being shouted at and cursed by drill instructors that did their best to make us tense and miserable. The DIs did one hell of a job, but who cared? I was going to fly. I was going to be an aviation cadet!

I qualified! I qualified right across the board as an accepted candidate for training as a pilot and/or navigator… as a PILOT!

They could still steal the deal from the bottom of the deck. The war, the BIG war, ended in 1945. I hadn't even made it up in a military airplane, flight school was still at another field and I hated those invisible people in Washington who cancelled the whole flight-training program. We, the sorely disappointed candidates, hung around like whipped dogs.

Life falters and stumbles, but it always begins anew if you're willing to never waste time feeling sorry for yourself. Feeling sorry for yourself is crazy, self-defeating and just plain stupid. In November of 1945, along with millions of other hopefuls, the Army Air Corps gave me my walking papers. I was back in the brilliant sunlight of civilian life although my sights were set. I hustled off to California where I enrolled in the Northrop Aeronautical Institute. There's not just another way to skin a cat, there's a whole book on the subject. I was cutting myself out a piece of the sky and this was now the best way to do the cutting. The moments in between hard studies and work came like scenes from a speeding motion picture.

I met Jeanne; light, lovely and radiant, and I knew somehow that our pasts had come together and we would share the rest of our lives in marriage… and we did. Those are the moments you'll never forget.

I watched, hypnotized, as Howard Hughes thundered low across the water lifting the gigantic wooden monster, *The Spruce Goose,* into the air. I was also privy, honored to be right there, I mean smack dab on the spot when the first huge Northrop XB-35 *Flying Wing* took to the skies. Here was a machine that looked as big as a football field and was all wing. It had monstrous thrashing propellers that made the deafening buzz saw sound of a tornado which could not be real; but it was real as it lifted into the heavens. Even then I knew I was witness to one of the true miracles of flight.

But back to the work of keeping the dreams and grasping the wonders. On the 30th of March in 1949, I did the smartest thing I ever did and married Jeanne Drain. That was my lucky star and as quickly as I could, I was back at the military volunteering once again to join the Aviation Cadet Program.

If I ever could have met the fellow called Fate who dealt from the bottom of the deck, I'd have killed him with my bare hands. All these years and suddenly I was disqualified to be an aviation cadet and a military pilot! Where had it come from? A severe malocclusion they called it, or just call it a rotten mouth. Jeanne and I scraped together every dime we had and I was off to the "medical facility," which is as good a name as any, for massive dental surgery. Afterwards I looked and felt like Paul Bunyan's ox had stomped me in the mouth and jaw, but those people knew what I was doing, and what they were doing, and repaired what nature had failed to do on its own. Everything now fit together and you can bet I was right back at the door of the military pounding hard and yelling to be allowed in.

The sun does come up. "You're in," was the word! I was almost able to levitate from the joy of it all, and having Jeanne there to share the victory made it all the sweeter.

*   *   *

I don't believe life is dissected neatly into chapters, as necessary as these may be in publishing a book about events, memories, and the things that meld together to constitute our history. That's tying everything together too neatly when in reality life slips from one phrase to another almost always overlapping just as incoming surf breaks over the water cascading along the bottom in the form of outgoing undertow. Yet, here I seemingly contradict myself because there are always those sharp breaks in the pattern, a stopping of much of what was a man's daily life and the entry into a whole new phase… or, to yield to the matter of publishing, the next chapter.

My sharp break came soon after those magic words… "You're in." One part of my life remained always unbroken and that was my marriage to Jeanne; that bond carried us through every new phase into which I now seemed to be hurtling faster and faster. It's as if you become not one, but several different minds, each attending to its own special niche.

With a new jaw and a renewed lease on life that spelled F-L-Y-I-N-G in dazzling neon lights across the centerpiece of my mind, I was off to Perrin Air Force Base in Sherman, Texas.

Now, if you take any experienced Air Force, Navy, or Marine pilot who was breaking free of the egg of his life in that period, you're going to find a pilot who tangled with the North American AT-6 Texan. Here was a brute of a trainer with 600 Clydesdales up front, square wings that could beat a D-8 bulldozer hands down, and had carefully designed into its characteristics just about every nasty habit an airplane could present to its cowed inhabitants. I had the advantage of already having flown, but in the long run, that mattered little.

Military training is doing it by the book; intense classroom study, disciplined flight training and mastering skills… demonstrated to final check pilots with claws, long teeth and red eyes who could flunk you out with a pitifully minor flick of a finger. Not here in this narration, but in the final story, the AT-6 deserves its special place. It's likely that more pilots learned to fly in this extraordinary plane than any other aircraft in military history.

I was gaining a new appreciation of what the demanding AT-6 wanted. It was the spokesman for all the military. We finally had a saying that you started off your 'hot bird' flying in a Grumman Hellcat; then you went from that pussycat to the bent winged and more demanding Vought F4-U Corsair, when you emerged from that 2,000 horsepower beast, you got into the snarly North American P-51 Mustang with its slippery laminar flow wing; an airplane that could bite you in a second of mistaken relaxation. When you'd mastered these three powerful brutes, you might be qualified to fly the Six (AT-6).

The new appreciation is simple to demonstrate. Recall, if you will, the dramatic histories of World War I with the Spad and Fokker, Rumpler and Camel, Nieuport and Gotha and then separate the best of the fighters. The AT-6, my first training airplane was as far advanced in power and performance over what the great Aces flew in the First World War as is the huge McDonnell-Douglas F-15 Eagle over my now ancient trainer.

I pounded through all the schools, took and passed all tests, demonstrated the flight proficiency that had my instructors perhaps a hair short of flinching badly… and was rewarded with orders to report to Advanced Flight School at Williams Air Force Base in Chandler, Arizona.

Jeanne and I could have waltzed the whole way because the only manner by which the military really tells you what they really think of you are those orders specifying your next assignment. Advanced flight training! The going was going to get tougher, but the airplanes would be quantum leaps forward with the flight envelopes expanding swiftly.

I was in hog heaven! From the 600 horsepower of the AT-6 smack into the cockpit of the bulky, stubby North American T-28 with double the power and verve. I had to keep reminding myself that when I flew the T-28 as a training airplane I was at the controls of a machine that outperformed the famed P-40 fighters of World War II.

I was far from being a snot-nosed neophyte brat, but the idea of flying fighter performance was heady wine indeed. Wham! No slacking off here! It was day and night training, studying and flying, becoming not merely proficient, but skilled. Maneuvering from ground level to miles into the heavens, flying in sun splashed skies and in miserable rain day and night into the aerobatics and routines that would enable me to become a skilled pilot; and a man who would fly a machine designed to shoot, strafe, hurl away rockets, drop bombs and rip the earth with blazing napalm.

In short, I was being taught, as are all fighter pilots, to become a professional killer. And you **know**, you absolutely **know** that you're the best-damned fighter pilot in the whole blamed world. We all believed that of ourselves. If you didn't, then the first time you went up against an enemy fighter pilot you were dead meat on the table and the odds were you'd never survive your first life and death engagement.

Everything was happening with greater speed. I sailed through advanced training in the thundering, bumping, clattering T-28 and was zipped onward and upward almost breathlessly into jet fighters, which was a whole new world of miraculous smoothness and power.

The F-80 Shooting Star and its two seat offspring, the T-33, were great-slick engines of energy. No whirling propeller, no vibration, as slick as any dolphin that ever cut through the water soaring upward and over. This is what great poets had written about and they were absolutely right. This was flying as no bird could fly. This was imagination brought from the mind to sleekness and power as a new magic carpet. I lavished in the sensational beauty of it all. Even now with guns, cannon, bombs and rockets there was that separation inside the cockpit.
There was first of all flight and everything else would have to follow behind.

How do you measure pride? Well… your buttons pop off your chest as you stand in a brace so tight you're like ramrod steel. Your wife is wringing her handkerchief into a sodden rag from her pride. You are both sharing it… and it's called Graduation Day! I stood strongly, fiercely, yet with a new inner calm born of new ability as the wings were pinned onto my chest.

It had been a long run from that cow pasture in North Carolina twenty years before. I drifted a few moments back in time as those silver wings went on my uniform and I swear I could hear the thunder of radial engines.
I could smell the oil and gasoline the five-year-old boy accepted with a devotion that would lead him across the years to this moment. I was out of the eggshell. I was a professional. The new life began…

The Air Force did not waste a moment putting one of their newest pilots to good use. Immediately after graduation, with my new wings gleaming on my uniform, I was assigned to overseas duty, with an interval delay assignment, to Nellis Air Force Base near Las Vegas, Nevada for fighter-gunnery training.

Nellis was all about learning how to shoot, how to bomb, how to launch rockets, salvo… to deliver weapons ordnance to enemy targets.

Of course there weren't any enemies in Nevada to be concerned about; we didn't shoot at coyotes and rabbits, but we did deliver our weapon loads against huge targets on the ground, against worn-out tanks, trucks, buildings and other equipment specifically laid out to receive our steadily increasing accuracy. This was further honing of the fighter pilot to be ready and able at a moment's notice to be sent on orders to a combat situation.

There was always one shadowy element that loomed distant but never forgotten. The Nevada desert was one of the major sites for testing the atomic bomb that was a weapon we all had to learn to live with. It might not have been dinner table conversation, but it rested deep in our minds that we too might be called upon one day to deliver such horrific devices in a future conflict. Make no mistake about it, not one pilot I ever knew wanted anything to do with such things, but nevertheless, we had to become proficient in the delivery of any weapon that might be necessary to defend this nation.

This rapid pace through fighter-gunnery training is but a whisper of the intense effort we went through in Nevada, of diving at ground targets, flying against mock enemies in the air, pulling g-forces and engaging in 'battles' that left us wrung out and worn to a frazzle by the end of a 'workday.'

When I left Nellis I was, without question, a member of the team that always stands at the forefront against danger to our country. It carried with it a swirling mixture of emotions. You become the best you can possibly be. You become a proficient artist in lethal weaponry... then hope

and pray that you'll never use your talents with intent to kill and destroy. It was the kind of hoping and praying that most of the world beyond our borders found laughable. My first overseas duty was intense. Intense is the best word to use for fighter pilot duty on the island of Okinawa. Not too many years earlier Okinawa had been the scene of savage battles and gruesome body counts between our combined military forces and fanatically fighting Japanese forces, in the final days of the Second World War.

Much of the devastation wrought in the struggle still pockmarked Okinawa yet we lived on a different emotional level working in the present and thinking toward the future. In this outline presentation, fierce activity, violent moments, and startling events can only take the form of vignettes.

I came within a split-second, or the hair of a dog might be more accurate, of being killed in the near fatal crash of my F-80 jet fighter on Yanton Air Base. Just staying on the ground on Okinawa could be more dangerous than flying!

We experienced the full force of a mighty typhoon savaging the island and the Asian coastline. The winds became so violent, at nearly 200 miles an hour, that the force blew apart buildings that filled the air with deadly shards of metal and huge sheets of flying shrapnel. It was almost my end when a sheet of corrugated metal, flung wildly through the air by the winds, missed decapitating me by bare seconds. It's the sort of thing that lets you know how really vulnerable we are to the whimsical touch of fate. That fickle finger you can never anticipate and the aftermath is always, if your IQ is higher than your neck size, a sweeter appreciation of life itself.

The lessons of life come unexpectedly in other ways. One of these lessons was the time I spent with a former pilot who had volunteered to die as a Kamikaze pilot. This Japanese man was quiet, reserved, and would never have been picked as someone so dedicated to his native land that he would hurl himself, as a human element of a "divine wind" against his country's' enemy.

Kamikazes had always been trumpeted in our press as suicide pilots. It was an incredible lesson to learn that suicide had nothing to do with willingly giving up your life so your people and your nation might survive. Duty to the death is not the same as suicide and simply goes a step beyond taking a dangerous risk. It was more than enlightening and made us wonder if we could do the same. The only reason this particular Kamikaze was still alive was because of mechanical failure rendering him unable to reach his enemy target… an American ship.

* * *

Remember the young fighter pilot fresh out of gunnery school training in the Nevada desert? That young man who, along with so many others, hoped and prayed he'd never have to use his sights on living targets. Well…all that went into the nearest trash can in June of 1950 when the North Koreans burst forth from their long-prepared positions along the 38th Parallel of the Korean peninsula, drove with devastating effect against the badly outnumbered American forces, and stunned the South Koreans.

Those of us on Okinawa and other stations knew it would soon be our turn to be sent into the fray.

That's what all the training had been for.
By late 1951, I was a new kind of fighter pilot; a veteran of fighter-bomber missions against North Korean and Chinese Communist forces on that forsaken peninsula.

The combat was intense, demanding and the enemy had some humongous anti-aircraft defenses to protect their powerful ground forces. On January 5th, 1952, I was diving against ground targets in the Kunuri area when my world disappeared in a roaring, blinding flash. My F-80 jet fighter took a direct hit! It tore the airplane apart and I barely got out of the once sleek jet that was no longer controllable. After successfully parachuting to the ground I did my best to get the hell away from the enemy forces closing in on me, but to no avail. I was captured almost immediately. Well… I'd been a combat pilot for only seventeen missions.

The long months that lay ahead after my capture has become a distant nightmare. But it takes only a moment to swirl away the time mists and recall with vivid detail my incredible time as a prisoner in the midst of an enemy that hardly any of us, the POWs, could understand; not only in language, but in mood, emotion and attitudes toward life itself. During those months of hunger, pain, threatened death again and again, I was grilled relentlessly by the enemy to bring me to confess to spreading deadly biological agents against the North Koreans and Chinese. Germ warfare was the name of the game they wanted in confessions and they were experts at brainwashing and physical degradation.

This was perhaps the most intensely human phase of my life because I was kept on the most base levels of survival and was hanging on grimly to the spirit that has served me well through life. It is a story mixing pain with relief. It's a story of hope with abject hopelessness upon so many around me. If there is anything that brought me, and most of the men with me, through the massive burden of the enemy trying to break us… it was faith. A faith in family, country and morality… whatever anyone wishes to call it. I cannot, in this brief space, give it proper intensity or meaning. But the story is different in its telling than anything I have ever seen in print, and is a triumph of spirit and faith against seemingly overwhelming odds.

New life begins in different ways. Obviously the life I knew was dumped unceremoniously into the nearest trash pile after I was shot down over enemy forces. That period of imprisonment, and all that wasted time, might as well have been lived on another planet. But finally it ended.

The war itself ground to a halt after tearing up the Korean countryside, killing and wounding hundreds of thousands of people. My role in that affair, in terms of physical involvement, ended when the prisoners of war were repatriated. After medical treatment and briefings, I could put the last two years behind me and look forward to a phase with succinct meaning... going home. But more than that; going home to Jeanne, to my family, to my country!

Aboard the troop ship (oh, how I wanted to FLY home!) we remained on maximum-alert war footing. Days and nights went by with infernal and frustrating slowness. The troop ships stayed off the main shipping lanes with strict radio silence maintained.

There was not only much sharing among the men aboard that ship, but also anger and no little hatred as well.

Two moments emerge as the strongest memories of that voyage. One American ex-POW had to be guarded constantly. His conduct as a prisoner of the enemy, witnessed by many other prisoners, was so sickening and hateful that, were he not guarded and protected, the ex-POWs would have immediately thrown him overboard. Comfort and aid to the enemy was, to us, outright treason. Had the opportunity been provided, that man would have never again set foot on what we considered the sacred soil of America.

There was one other moment when the urge to kill welled up in so many of us. I had collected one hundred and twenty names of fellow prisoners in a notebook. I had written down the names and other information in urine so upon my return to the States I could notify families that these men were still alive.

An inept, idiotic, unbelievably stupid Army "Intelligence" officer paid scant attention to my notebook… and destroyed it along with all the intensely emotional names and personal data it contained! You don't need more than one guess to know who the second man the POWs wanted to throw to the sharks.

What goes around comes around, is an old saying often reflecting tradition rather than accuracy. But somehow it remains imbued with surprising accuracy. After rather intense medical checkups and recovery from idle problems such as malnutrition, bruises and battering at the hands of my unfriendly hosts in Korea, and especially after spending healing time with my family, the *comes around* brought me back to Nellis Air Force Base in Nevada.

There are always differences when you return somewhere after a long absence. I first landed at Nellis as a brand new pilot with wings too new to tarnish. I'd learned the art of gunnery, bombing and rocketing there. At least I'd flown seventeen missions impelled by that training.

The neophyte was now gone. In the eyes of the Air Force I was now an experienced, hardened veteran which placed me in the position of leading and training the new comers who arrived at Nellis… new comers as I had once been. I became an instructor pilot in perhaps the sweetest flying jet fighter ever made; the sweeping F-86 Sabre. Permit me my opinion, for every now and then a dream airplane comes along that is so beautifully responsive and perfectly balanced that it makes its pilot lord and master of the sky.

Well… lord and master is a relative term of course. But dancing along wisps of clouds, flying effortlessly, you wonder if the birds are envying you in all the beauty. The experiences in the F-86 dissolved much of the recent unpleasant experience.

I slipped into another new world when I took off on my first flight in the successor to the F-86; the brutish, powerful, heavy F-100 Super Sabre. The F-100 was the first jet able to slam through the sound barrier and sustain level flight at supersonic speed and I moved quickly through my entry into the world of flying faster than sound.

 I was experiencing the heady mixture of having what every pilot wants to have beneath his hands and instructing new comers to Nellis. I moved quickly upward through the demanding levels of disciplined flight and performance. I grabbed the brass ring… two of them in fact! The first was meeting the standards to become a member of the Nellis Weapons Team which was a position reached only through razor sharp performance.

I now slide through a major phase of my life and into a dream that I would never have thought could be even remotely possible. I was tested, flown against, studied and analyzed… and was chosen to become a member of the famed *Thunderbirds* jet demonstration team that was renowned for precision aerobatics and silky maneuvers. The *Thunderbirds* were flying the F-100 that we all called the 'lead sled.'

The *Thunderbirds* are a complete world unto themselves traveling about the planet and flying before millions of people. We were again away from home and family for perhaps 320 days a year. We were heroic celebrity figures, signing autographs, attending endless social functions and frankly, flying our butts to the painful point.

If ever we became just a bit smug, we were always put back in our place by the *Thunderbird* wives upon our return to Nellis. In our minds we were the returning heroes sliding from the sky in our supersonic fighters. But to the wives it was… "Here come those horny bastards with their dirty laundry!" …which is the perfect, all-too-true comedown!

There is a moment with the *Thunderbirds* to be expanded in the book. A faux pas on my part that is one of the deadliest of social sins that instantly branded me, amongst the world flying community, as the cause of an international incident involving a highly ranked figure of a foreign government. The only saving grace from near-disaster was the hysterical laughter of my fellow pilots, plus the jibes and barbs that came my way in a thick cloud. All too deserved… I freely admit.

I never dreamed of cruising above most of the atmosphere of this planet and I had never heard of the U-2. Despite my Top Secret Clearance, and the clearance of my fellow pilots, we were never permitted to get even close to a secret base isolated far out in the Nevada desert. But that base would become as familiar to me as was Nellis when a fellow pilot, oh so cleverly and so smoothly, duped me into accepting an assignment I doubt I would have ever knowingly accepted.

This put me fourteen miles high over the Soviet Union with the world teetering on the brink of nuclear war and the President of the United States enraged at that "son of a bitch" he believed was too thick between the ears to know he should not be offending the angry, volatile Russians by flying over their homeland. I, in effect, was thumbing my nose at the best of their fighters and missiles.

My God... I almost was the cause of World War Three!

The adventuring about the planet in the U-2 is sufficient unto itself to fill and entire book with chair gripping excitement and historical revelations. It has a major niche in my life story. But once again, it was but a phase into another era-rife with excitement and violent flying always a short jump ahead of the Grim Reaper.

Then along came yet another war. Would they never end? I left behind the upper stratospheric heights and the Presidential name-calling and entered the cockpit of yet another mighty brute, the successor to the F-100, the huge F4-C Phantom II jet fighter. It was designated a fighter, but it was actually a double supersonic monster, larger and heavier than a medium bomber in World War II armed with a pillaging Viking's dream of terrible weapons. It could carry a greater bomb load than even the four-engine B-17 Flying Fortress that destroyed our enemies during World War II.

Sometimes I would stand off mentally from myself and see that five-year old kid climbing into the Ford Tri-motor... Incredible!

Chapter 1

The Bad Boyhood

I was the fourth child of six, born on the 7th of June, 1926 in Greenville, North Carolina to Isaac Wayne Maultsby, a shoe maker by trade, and Cecelia Lash. There is little I remember from birth to 1931 other than my family seemed to be constantly moving from one place to another until we settled in Greensboro, North Carolina in 1931. I remember that my father always seemed to be on the road looking for work. He only came home once or twice a month for a day or two, and then he was off again on his motorcycle.

I found out years later while talking with my older sisters, Margaret and Inez, that those were very rough times, where my mother often had as little as seventy-five cents a week to feed five children (my older brother died at birth). Nevertheless those were happy times to a five year old. I reflect back now and realize how many sacrifices she must have made for us, doing without herself, so we could have special treats occasionally. Simple things, like an ice cream cone after a Saturday afternoon walk. I remember telling her one day, "When I grow up I'm going to buy you all the ice cream you can eat!" She smiled and patted my shoulder.

Mom worked from sunup to sundown, but I can remember her setting aside the time to play with us each day. We would all take turns choosing our favorite games. We all seemed to have plenty to eat and clothes on our backs. This, I learned later, was the result of the generosity of my maternal grandmother who lived in Portsmouth, Virginia with my mother's sister Inez and Uncle Louis. On occasion my grandmother would visit and, as if by magic, the electric lights would work. But soon after she left, out they would go.

We lived in a small two bedroom frame house with no plumbing. There was a wood burning stove in the kitchen, a dining room, and a living room with a fireplace. Wood for the stove and fireplace was provided by the transient Hobos who were frequent visitors to our home during the depression years. I looked forward to their visits and the stories they told of their travels. They were always welcome to share whatever food we had, and some even brought fresh vegetables that I now suspect were liberated from the surrounding farms. We never once felt threatened by these men who were down on their luck; which would not be the case today. They knew a good thing when they saw it and even went so far as to mark the curb in front of our house with chalk to let other transients know a meal was awaiting them.

It was during our stay in Greensboro when I first became aware that there was such a thing as an airplane. One flew low over our house and scared me and my sisters. My mother settled us down and explained as best she could what the contraption was all about. From then on I looked forward to seeing, what I believed to be, the same plane I first saw flying over our house and always in the same direction.

I later learned that it was a mail plane. I learned more about airplanes after I entered the first grade and was privy to books on Lindberg, WW I fighter pilots, and the mail planes. My mother and older sisters would read to me until I believe they became experts on the subject of airplanes.

Things improved financially or the family that last year we lived in Greensboro, so much so that my father was able to buy an automobile. He still was working out of town, but he came home now and then. We all looked forward to a Sunday ride in the little coupe with the rumble seat. It was during one of these outings that we approached a pasture that had several airplanes plus a weird looking craft with no wings and a huge fan on top that turned out to be a Kellet autogyro.

After much urging by my sisters and me, my father finally consented to stopping to have a look at all the flying machines; not that he was the least bit interested. The one craft that especially appealed to me was a large metal plane with three engines, one on the nose and one on each wing. It turned out to be a Ford Tri-motor, some of which are still in service today.

After running all around this great beauty and marveling that anything this big and heavy could actually fly, there was an announcement over a loud speaker that it was preparing to take passengers up for a sightseeing ride. I remember the fare being two or three dollars a head… which meant absolutely nothing to me and I was determined to wheedle it out of my father. He didn't go for the idea, and I'm sure my mother had something to do with him finally giving in.

To this day I can recall every moment of that flight; starting with my being lifted up into the door way by a fellow passenger who buckled me into a wicker seat and became my companion for the next twenty minutes.

While waiting for the other passengers to be seated I was fascinated by all of the different smells; gasoline, hydraulic fluid, oil and others of unknown origin. Finally I heard the door close. A man walked up the aisle, pausing long enough to give me a pat on the shoulder, and then proceed to the little cabin where all the strange dials and gadgets were located. It seemed like an eternity before the first engine coughed into life and it wasn't long before all three we singing the same tune.

The plane seemed to tremble as if it were anxious to get on with it. There was a delay while the pilots were busy checking things. Finally they were satisfied with whatever they were doing. The next thing I knew the plane started moving ever so slowly, gaining speed as the engines changed their tune to a dull roar.

The pasture was very rough causing the plane to rock back and forth, and up and down all at the same time. I felt confident that the pilot knew what he was doing, but wondered why we seemed to be wandering all over the pasture. Finally he found a spot he liked and brought the big plane to a stop.

"Now what," I wondered when all of a sudden the engines gave off a powerful roar! We started going faster and faster until suddenly I felt the back of the plane come up. The bounces came more frequently then suddenly... nothing. It felt as if the plane was suspended and the earth seemed to fall away. It was a sensation I couldn't have described back then, but I have experienced it many times since with the same exhilaration.

We climbed higher and higher until the houses and farmland below looked like something constructed in a sand pile. I was puzzled by how slow we seemed to be going, comparing it to the speed with which the mail planes seemed to zip by.

Suddenly the whole plane rolled over to execute a turn, giving me the frightening sensation of possibly falling out the window, and continued the turn for what seemed like an eternity! Then, as suddenly as it had started, the plane rolled back to an upright position. I settled back determined to soak in the many sensations that I felt I would probably never experience again.

My daydreaming was interrupted as the plane started rolling in the other direction causing me to fear that I would fall into the aisle. About this time the engines became quieter. Looking out the window across the aisle I could tell that we were getting lower and lower and turning all the while. I recognized the pasture with all the airplanes and was sure that that was where we were going. The plane rolled back to the normal position so I could no longer see the pasture.

Looking out a window it appeared as if we were going to land in an approaching group of trees. There was a bump, followed by more bumps and I realized that we were on the same rough pasture that we left just minutes ago. As the plane slowed, the back end started to drop ever so slightly accompanied by another bump. This time the pilot didn't meander all over the pasture, but instead he quickly stopped and the plane and the engines became silent.

I left the plane with mixed emotions and hoped even then that there would be more experiences with these fascinating contraptions. How much more only God knew. That Sunday in an unknown pasture would help shape the rest of my life. Although it would be ten years before I would take flight again.

The next thing I knew we were on the move again. This time to Danville, Virginia where my father opened a shoe repair shop. The year: 1934, the darkest year of my life.

We moved to Danville sometime during the summer, but I remember little else about this move other than the house we rented was a large two story white frame located near a brick church. My sisters and I were enrolled in school and everything was rosy for the Maultsby clan… until a visit from our grandmother turned our whole world upside down.

My sisters and I sensed that something very strange was occurring when we overheard my father, mother and grandmother talking about taking a trip to Norfolk immediately. We assumed that another move was about to take place, but this was not the case.

My grandmother had come to visit and became enraged when she discovered that my mother had a goiter as large as a grapefruit on her neck. She recognized it instantly and began calling my father every name in the book for his negligence by not seeking medical attention.

My grandmother called Inez and Louis in Norfolk and asked them to come immediately. They were there the next day to whisk our mother away without much explanation other than she needed an operation. Not fully understanding what an operation was, combined with the urgency of actions, gave my sisters and me a feeling of despair. We went through the motions of everyday life, but none of us could concentrate in school and we withdrew into our own little shells.

Approximately one week after our mother left, my father called us all together and told us our mother died on the operating table on the 20th of September, 1934, just the day before. No words I knew of then, or now, can describe how we felt. We weren't allowed to cry because our father considered crying a sign of weakness.

We were at a complete loss when it struck home we would never see our mother again. My sisters and I went our separate ways; to closets, the bathroom, and I went to a shed outside. Once alone I could no longer hold back the tears that welled up inside me… "He won't be able to hear me out here!" A total feeling of desolation, and then despair, swept over me. I sat sobbing in the dark shed. I thought of another day with my father when I was thrown into total darkness.

My father prided himself on being a great outdoorsman who could live off the land like the fabled mountain men. He would take hikes through the wilderness always going in a straight line, over and under, but never around an obstacle. One Sunday he took me on one of his hikes.

He maintained a brisk walk not allowing for my short steps. We came to a river, not more than fifty feet across, that he proceeded into and directed me to follow him. It was a swift moving, muddy river, that made it more frightening, and he was already shoulder deep.

I thought, "No, he really won't make me do this… I can't swim!" The thought made me tremble and I started to cry. I saw the look of disgust as he waded ashore. He approached quickly and grabbed me by the hand. I tried desperately to pull away from him, but I was no match for his strength.

He led me to a bridge about two hundred yards upstream. I continued to struggle, then realized that we were already about half way across the bridge. The next few moments were so terrifying I lost my breath.

I was being flung over the side of the bridge rail; it seemed like an eternity until my body hit the water. I felt myself sinking deeper into the inky black water finally hitting bottom. I instinctively began thrashing my arms and legs, which brought me to the surface. In my panic I tried to keep my head above the water. I was moving quickly with the current thrashing wildly all the while. Miraculously I was swept up onto a bank. I'd taken in a lot of water, so I lay with my face down, choking and coughing, while desperately trying to catch my breath. I became aware that my father was leaning over the bridge rail laughing.

He had watched my struggling from that vantage point and made no effort to help. I then heard him yell, "You little sissy!"

It was a cold and rainy day when my Aunt and Uncle came for my sisters and me to make the trip to Portsmouth, Virginia. It was anything but pleasant staying with my Aunt and Uncle awaiting my mother's funeral. The day of the funeral there were many people gathered in the funeral parlor, most of whom I'd never seen before, but we were somehow related.

Our little world now took on a new meaning. I heard some of them say over and over, "God rest her soul, she's better off where she is." I couldn't understand why anyone would say such a thing about the sweetest, kindest, person who ever walked the earth. I understand now, but it took many years after that day to figure it out… and accept it.

Events happened fast after the funeral. My Aunt and Uncle, who were childless, felt they were incapable of housing five children; and our father felt the same way.

Arrangements were made to enroll my four sisters in Saint Joseph's Villa, a boarding school for girls, in Richmond, Virginia. I was to return to Danville, Virginia with my father. Upon our return, I was surprised when we drove up to the very house where I last saw my mother alive. The memories were more than an eight year old boy should have to bear.

My father hired a housekeeper who moved in with her two children, who were about my age, but this arrangement didn't last long. My father terminated the housekeeper's employment and we then moved out of the house and into the back of his shoe repair shop. It was not home sweet home. The accommodations consisted mostly of store rooms, a cot, toilet, a sink but no bathing facilities.

We occasionally bathed at the YMCA where I found it shocking to see grown men and boys parading around naked… even in the swimming pool.

My father's business seemed to be doing well with more customers than he could accommodate. He hired more help and even opened a shoe shine stand employing a black man to run it. The shoeshine stand provided a light, in an otherwise dark existence, because it was manned by the nicest gentleman I had ever met. His son was about twelve and we became the best of friends.

I enrolled in the third grade in the same school that my sisters had attended but it wasn't long before the teachers and the principal agreed that I wasn't keeping up with the other children. They notified my father and suggested that he hire a tutor, or they would have to send me back to the second grade.

The tutor he hired through the classifieds turned out to be a jewel that took a special interest in me and instilled some much needed self-confidence. Things were going well. I looked forward to school and I enjoyed the tutoring sessions after school. Then, as suddenly as they began, the tutoring sessions stopped. And my father didn't hire another tutor.

True to their word, my teachers and principal recommended that I be returned to the second grade. But fate played a role that prevented this from happening. My father and I returned to the same house that we recently left and he hired another housekeeper. I no longer attended school whiling away my time in movie theaters and shooting galleries.

I became so proficient with a 22 caliber rifle that my father took bets that I could outshoot all comers; and won most of those bets.

Just before Christmas, in 1934, my father instructed the housekeeper to have me bathed and dressed in my finest clothes because we would be taking a trip. He usually arrived from work at around 6:00 pm.

I was ready by 5:00, but made the mistake of going outside to do some rough housing with a couple of playmates. Minutes before I thought my father would arrive, I hurried into the house to clean up… but it was too late. He was standing in the kitchen. He took one look at me and flew into a rage. He grabbed me by the left arm and started whaling away on my backside with such force that my feet left the floor after each whack. I thought to myself, "Don't cry, just don't cry or this will never stop."

Finally my bladder and my bowels let go simultaneously. I was wearing short pants, so the next whack splattered urine and feces on his trousers. He flung me across the room with such force that the wall knocked the wind out of me… but I didn't cry. He then stomped out of the kitchen.

The house keeper helped me up off of the floor and steered me into the bathroom upstairs. She knew better than to interfere when he was in one of his moods. By the time my father and I were cleaned up there was no time left to have dinner, so we left in silence headed for the train station. I had no idea where we were going.

He didn't say one word to me until we arrived at our destination, which turned out to be Norfolk where my Aunt

Inez and Uncle Louis were waiting to greet us. I couldn't help but notice the tense silence during the trip from the train station to 520 Connecticut Ave. I later learned that my relatives were not on friendly terms.

The next day I learned the reason for the trip to Norfolk. The little country bumpkin, me, was now entering another chapter in his life.

My Aunt and Uncle asked me if I would like to come live with them on Christmas Eve. I didn't think they were fond of children and was surprised by the question.

However, they did have a comfortable home that looked a lot better than what I had just left. My father didn't have anything to say; so I thought it had already had been arranged. I accepted their offer with reluctance, but what does an eight year old know?

As it turned out, it was one of the most important decisions I'd ever make. God only knows what kind of a future would have awaited me had I stayed with my father.

Christmas morning I awakened to find more toys and clothes than I ever imagined could exist. I was dumb-founded to say the least. The thought occurred to me that my Aunt and Uncle knew well in advance that I would accept their offer.

I don't recall my father's leaving and I had no way of knowing that it would be eight years before I would see him again… and that was fine with me.

Chapter 2

The Budding Pilot

The next ten years would prove to be the turning point in my life. Although it was impossible to compensate for the loss of my mother, there were two companions, other than my Aunt and Uncle, who made life a joy; my Grandmother and our maid, Maggie. My Aunt and Uncle both worked; he for a brass and copper concern as a secretary treasurer, and she as a secretary at an insurance company. My Grandmother and Maggie cared for me, loved me, and performed all the duties of stay at home moms.

My Aunt told me I reminded my Grandmother of her son, my Uncle Patsy. He was wounded, gassed, and later captured by the Germans in World War I. My Grandmother didn't like to talk about Patsy, but she did say he was well treated by the Germans. When he returned home from the war he suffered the after effects of the gassing. It was one of those after effects that took his life.

He died on a Saturday while preparing to meets some friends to attend a football game. He'd just finished a bath, when he lost consciousness while getting out of the tub and fell against a gas heater. My Grandmother was the one who found him, which may help to explain her reluctance to discuss her beloved son.

Perhaps I did remind my Grandmother of Patsy, because occasionally she would call me Patsy without realizing it. I think it was through me that she had a part of him back.

I don't know how long Maggie worked for my Aunt and Uncle before I came to live with them, but she was certainly treated as a member of the family. She was a most pleasant lady who doted on me as if I were her own son. She always cooked my favorite dishes, pies, and cakes while still attending to her normal chores.

She worked five and a half days a week doing all the cooking, cleaning, washing, ironing, and all the other chores a housekeeper did in those days. She did all of this for $5 a week plus bus and ferry fare. She lived in Portsmouth, across the James River from Norfolk, which necessitated a ferry ride to Norfolk, and then a bus ride each day to Colonial Place where we lived. I don't remember her ever missing a day come rain or shine.

My school days began anew with the new year of 1935. My Aunt enrolled me in the J.E.B. Stuart Elementary School five blocks from our house. My first day gave me the impression that I didn't belong. Most of my class all grew up in the same neighborhood and seemed to resent a Carolina hick in their midst.

Having never experienced a prejudiced environment before, I became a loner. I only looked forward to going home after school where my circle of friendly faces would happily welcome me.

My Aunt was my tutor and a strict one at that, but it didn't take her long to realize that I wasn't cutting the muster. I barely made the grade and finished out the school year more miserable than ever.

The following year my Aunt enrolled me at Sacred Heart Elementary School knowing that the Sisters of Charity were the ones who could pound some sense into me. My Mother and Aunt were raised in a Catholic school for girls.

Those Sisters did pound on me for the next five years. I'm sure I could have been entered in the Guinness Book of Records for having the most oak wood pointers broken over my head. Between the Sisters and my Aunt Inez, the "little hick" shaped up somewhat, but I didn't attain scholarly status.

Colonial Place was ideally situated for a growing boy who enjoyed the outdoors. It was located on the Lafayette River, a tributary of the James River. This environment provided many happy hours fishing, crabbing and swimming in the Lafayette's murky water.

Across the river was a dirt strip airport not more than a fifteen minute bike ride from our house. I visited the little airport often, spending hours ogling the few private planes hangered there while eves dropping in on the pilots and mechanics as they discussed their businesses.

They ignored me at first, but as my visits became more frequent they acknowledged me a bit. I made it a point not to wear out my welcome by being in the way, but I stayed close enough to watch an engine being overhauled, or a wing being re-covered. Try hanging around an airport now days just to see how long it will take to be asked to leave.

One aircraft I particularly liked was a Stinson Reliant. It was state of the art in its day, but even by today's standards, it's a beautiful machine that I saw recently restored to mint condition.

One Saturday, during a visit to the little airport, the owner of the Stinson was waxing and polishing his pride and joy; I asked him if I could help. He gladly accepted my offer and hinted that he might take me up for a flight someday. I waxed and polished that beautiful machine until my hands were raw. Sometime later, the owner indeed took me up for a flight.

The Norfolk Naval Air Station provided a wealth of aircraft for an aspiring aviator to examine and observe as they shot touch and go landings. Before the war there was no problem gaining access to the Air Station, visitors were welcome. I would often ride a street car to the main gate then head directly for the flight line where there were dive-bombers, torpedo bombers, flying boats and fighter planes. I was fascinated with them all, but I particularly liked the little fighter planes.

The fighters were the stubby Grumman F3Fs that looked like they could hold their own in a scrap. On one occasion I was fortunate enough to talk to one of the F3F pilots who allowed me to sit in the cockpit.

He damaged his tail wheel, while shooting touch and go landings, and was waiting for the maintenance crew to repair it. I kept him company for the hours it took to make the repair. He was part of a squadron that had been at sea for months. It was a common practice for carrier based planes to take off while still forty to fifty miles from port to practice landings on land. Before the war, fleet arrivals were announced well in advance, so I knew when to camp out at the auxiliary strip to watch them practice.

It was during the years around 1937 to 1939 that I decided I was going to be a naval pilot. I informed my Aunt and Uncle who were non-committal, figuring I would surely change my mind many times, as most kids do. They pointed out that I would first have to graduate from Annapolis if I wanted to earn the golden wings of a Navy flyer. I would have to do extremely well in high school and compete with thousands of other applicants to secure an Annapolis appointment.

I graduated from Sacred Heart Elementary School in June 1937 and enrolled in Holy Trinity High School the following fall only because most of my classmates did so. That was a big mistake, or so I thought at the time.

There were one hundred and twenty students enrolled at Holy Trinity that prepared students for careers in anything but the military. I figured correctly that four years of math and science would be more beneficial to me than four years of Latin and religion. I mentioned to my Aunt and Uncle that I wanted to transfer to a public school, but was overruled.

The Sisters of the Holy Cross had a reputation for turning out young men and women who became leaders in their chosen field. It was difficult to concentrate on my studies when the news was mostly reporting the war brewing in Europe. It seemed that I would never attend Annapolis, or any other academy, so I directed my attention toward a career in civil aviation.

I worked after school as a theater usher, soda jerk, drugstore delivery boy and whatever else came up.

While working at the drug store, a young man mentioned a private airport that offered flying lesson for eight bucks an hour. He had accumulated enough hours to be tested for his private pilot license and asked me if I wanted to go with him the next Saturday for his check flight. I immediately accepted his offer, my boss gave me the day off, and it was agreed that I would be picked up at 8 a.m. by my new friend, Joe. His flight was scheduled for 10:30 on that magical Saturday morning.

Joe was there on time as promised and we drove fourteen miles to the Glenrock airport in his '37 Plymouth. I was very impressed with this man who had amassed a total of forty hours flying time. I bombarded him with questions that he patiently answered, but was probably becoming sorry that he'd brought me along.

We arrived at Glenrock airport that was similar to the airport near our house in Norfolk. It consisted of a grass "T" shaped runway, a 12 ft. X 12 ft. operations shack, and two small wooden hangers. Joe left me to look around while he met with the instructor to brief for his check flight. There were six J-3 Piper Cubs and a Fleet bi-plane, powered by a Kenner radial engine, there that day.

No one seemed to mind my being around, so I inspected the hangers that I thought were a disgrace. There were motor and airplane pieces scattered everywhere in the dirt floor amongst the trash and oily rags. It made me wonder about the airworthiness of the planes.

I wandered into the operations shack to inquire about taking lessons even though I was broke. I'd worry about that later. I was informed I would need a physical, in order to obtain a student permit, and eight hours of lessons to solo... if my proficiency permitted. Asking my Aunt and Uncle for sixty dollars was out of the question; I didn't think they would approve of my taking flying lessons anyway.

I'd have to work all the after school hours I could, plus a half day on Saturdays, and save every penny to pay for lessons myself. I never saw Joe again after his flight check at the Glenrock airport that Saturday morning. I heard he joined the Army Air Corps.

I rode my bike the twenty eight mile round trip to Glenrock airport on Saturdays where I amassed ten hours in the venerable J-3 Piper Cub. My first lesson was more than I hoped it would be; which was a basic orientation flight following the instructor through on the controls. My instructor, Sparky Harris, allowed me to fly the Cub straight and make a few turns which was just enough to further whet my appetite for flying. Sparky was impressed that I had memorized the pre-flight checks.

I quickly learned procedures such as starting the engine, warm-up, taxi, take off, air work, approach and landing. He was a stickler for maintaining heading, altitude, and airspeed, which all together, taxed my abilities. But after a few more flights I felt more at ease and progressed rapidly. I enjoyed the landing phase the most; when Sparky would point to a spot on the field and order me to, "Touch down there!" I had to wait for my sixteenth birthday to solo and did so on June 7th 1942.

It was the last flight I would make for another three years. The war caused Glenrock airport to close, and all J-3 Cubs were being turned over to the Civil Air Patrol for coastal patrol.

I spent the summer of 1943 at my Grandfather's (Uncle Louis' father) beach house in Ocean View, Virginia. It was there I saw, and experienced, the reality of war. For several days a huge convoy had been forming in the Chesapeake Bay consisting of, at least, one hundred and fifty ships, all shapes and sizes, riding at anchor.

I was fishing in a little row boat, about two hundred yards off shore, when I heard a muffled explosion, followed by two more. I looked up to see two large ships engulfed in flames and smoke. When the smoke drifted away, those ships had disappeared.

The newspaper accounts the next day speculated that a German U-boat had somehow gotten through the anti-submarine nets stretched from Little Creek to Cape Charles. On several occasions U-boats followed ships through the nets to wreaked havoc on U.S. ships.

Three days after the sinking of the two ships I was swimming about fifty yards off shore and bumped into what I thought was a porpoise; which wasn't a fright because porpoise are friendly. I looked below the surface and then experienced a fright! What I had bumped into was the body of a crew member from one of those ships that were torpedoed. I hailed a passing motor boat and we took the body ashore. The unfortunate fellow couldn't have been much older than me.

The waters off the coast of Virginia were happy hunting grounds for German U-boats during the summer of 1943. A family friend was a crew member on a tanker who would sometimes stay with my Grandfather and me when his ship was in port. He was probably in his early thirties and had been all over the world; having gone to sea in his late teens. We became pals and spent many happy times together during his time off duty. The last day I spent with him before he shipped out was spent fishing, followed by a fish fry I'll never forget… he was one hell of a cook!

The next day I watched his convoy depart and murmured a little prayer for his safe voyage. A day later the newspaper account mentioned that his ship and two others had been U-boat victims. There were no survivors.

I started my last year at Holy Trinity High in the fall of 1943. There wasn't much to look forward to, as far as flying was concerned, except an occasional visit to the Norfolk Municipal Airport. It had become a P-47 transition school for the Army Air Corps. The pilots were then assigned to operational units in the European Theater. I would have given my eye teeth to trade places with one of those pilots. I didn't know it then, but that was exactly what I had to do to get those silver wings.

The Army and Navy's need for pilots opened the door for those of us who might never have had the chance to apply and be accepted for flight school. The Navy had a program called V-5 that required at least two years of college to qualify. The Army Air Corps had a more flexible program that allowed high school students to apply for the Pre-Aviation Cadet program.

Applicants were required to pass a battery of comprehensive tests, pass a flight physical, and be interviewed by a psychiatrist. You were then sworn in as a Pre-Aviation Cadet to be called up upon your eighteenth birthday. The opportunity this program offered was an answer to my prayers, but I couldn't help but worry about the battery of tests. I hoped the questions would be related to religion and Latin.

Fortunately, the questions were mostly about problem solving using common sense. The local Army recruiter made my appointment to take the tests at Langley Field in Hampton, VA.

I was very nervous when I hopped on the streetcar on Granby Street that took me to the ferry dock in Willoughby. The ferry to Hampton took thirty minutes; from there I took a shuttle bus to Langley Field and was let off near the officers club. From there it was a short walk to where I was to report.

On the way I passed some of the most beautiful English Tudor style homes I'd ever seen. They were two story duplexes with slate roofs and were surrounded by ancient magnolia trees. I stopped a moment to study a particular duplex. I wondered what it would be like to be an Army Air Corps officer and live in a nice house like that.

Several fellow aspiring aviators were assembled in the personnel office when I arrived. Several test booklets were passed out to be completed in a given time frame. My heart palpitated and my mouth went dry as I opened the first booklet and began reading.

The first questions were simple, but they became steadily difficult. When time was up I hadn't answered all the questions in the last booklet, and felt I hadn't passed.

Upon comparing notes with my fellow applicants, I found out most didn't even get to the last test booklet. The results would arrive in the mail in a week or so. A physical was next for those who passed.

The next week was the longest of my life. I wasn't home the day the "life or death" letter arrived from Langley. Maggie knew how much I was looking forward to the letter and handed it to me as soon as I got home. I sat down but couldn't make myself open it. Maggie opened it for me, read it, and then handed it back with a sly grin on her face.

Her grin told me that it was good news and sure enough… I had passed with flying colors! I was instructed to report to the base hospital on a particular day and time to undergo the physical and psychiatric exams. I wondered what these exams would be like, never having had a physical or psychiatric evaluation before.

I examined a brochure I'd been given during my first application outlining the criteria for qualifying for flight status. Some of the criteria included sound physical and mental health, high moral standards, minimum/maximum height and weight… Uh Oh! The minimum weight was 135 pounds and after weighing myself, I was only 130 pounds!

Maggie convinced me that by eating bananas prior to the weigh-in I could gain a few pounds. Plus I had a week to fatten up. The minimum height was another problem. You had to be at least five feet two inches. Maggie measured me at five feet one and a half inches! How could I possibly grow a half inch in a week?

Uncle Louis suggested that I go hang from the chinning bar in the garage as long as I could every day…, which I did to the point of pain. But when the day of the physical came I was still only 132 pounds… and I hadn't grown at all. I had asked my Aunt to pick up six pounds of bananas on her way home from work the night before the exam.

I ate all six pounds on the ferry ride to Hampton; I don't recall ever eating another one.

I arrived at the Langley Field hospital on time and was greeted by the smiling faces of some of the fellas who had taken the written test with me. We all were ordered to strip to our shorts and socks, and follow the signs from one exam room to the next.

We were split up into two groups to expedite things, and were sent in opposite directions. I was in the group that would be weighed and measured first. So being the runt, I let all the other fellas go first, hoping that I would be overlooked; until a stern corpsman motioned me to the scale. He adjusted the weights down, down, and on down to 136… made it! Then he lowered the horizontal bar down for the height measurement until it rested on my head. He seemed to hesitate for an eternity, then he shouted, "Stand up straight!" He also placed his thumb strategically on my spine with such force that the bar read 5 feet 6 inches. He then called out; "Next!" …there are some wonderful people on this earth.

The rest of the physical took about an hour for the fifteen of us. Everything was going well until the dentist who examined me declared that I had a severe malocclusion (overbite), but it wouldn't disqualify me from flight status. Whew! I'd never thought about my teeth. When we were finished with our physicals, we assembled in a clinic next to the hospital to wait for our name to be called in alphabetical order.

When called, you entered a small room and sat across from a kindly looking Major seated behind his desk. He asked a lot of questions, such as, why I wanted to join the Army, did I ever think about being killed, and so forth. I answered the best I could. After ten minutes of questioning he rose, extended his hand, and wished me luck in the P-51. And that's the extent of my first experience with a psychiatrist.

Some other fellas volunteered that they were asked rather shocking questions such as; "would you rather have intercourse with your mother or sister,"
or "have you ever sodomized an animal?" I wondered why I hadn't been asked similar questions…

When the last interview was done, we were directed back to the main hospital to receive further instructions. We were informed we would be notified by mail regarding the test results. Those who passed would report to Langley Field to be sworn in as Army Pre-Aviation Cadets to be called to active duty after passing our eighteenth birthday.

Another anxious week lay ahead waiting for results. I reviewed the tests in my head to anticipate the results; eyes were 20-20, blood pressure good, height and weight OK, spread cheeks OK, pulse OK, so it must be blood and urine tests that could ruin me. I couldn't rule out the psychiatric exam either; maybe I wasn't asked "kooky" questions for a reason that would disqualify me.

There was much to worry about. The war was passing me by and when it ended; my chance at an aviation career would end. All flight training programs would be shut down for who knows how long.

I waited three weeks for the official looking letter that came from Langley Field. This time Maggie didn't have to read it first. I ripped it open and read the first word, which was, "Congratulations." I was ecstatic as I read the rest of the letter and at the bottom were blanks that hand been filled in by hand:

Report   NLT   0900   25 March, 1944 ...etc.

Aunt Inez and Uncle Louis were happy for me, but I sense that my Aunt had reservations; probably because of what happened to her brother Patsy in WW I. She also knew that I would be eligible for the draft in a few months, flight training took a year, during which time the war could end.

The day arrived that ended my civilian status until the end of the war. Uncle Louie let me use his 1940 Ford sedan for the trip to Langley Field. I arose at 4:00 a.m. on the 25th of March, 1944, giving myself plenty of time to get ready for the drive.

I arrived with time to kill, and went directly to the building where the oath would be taken. There were a few military personnel in the halls, but the adjutant's office was locked. I recognized six other guys dressed in civilian clothes.

They had passed the tests and were there to be sworn in too.

The adjutant arrived at 0730 and asked us to be seated around a large table. A civilian secretary passed out several forms to be filled out. This done, the adjutant asked us to stand and raise our right hands. He administered the military oath, shook each of our hands, wished us the best of luck, and presented each of us a Pre Aviation Cadet certificate and PAC lapel pin.

June 6th 1944 was D-Day. It was also the day before my eighteenth birthday. My being called up was close; there were things to be done, such as visiting my two younger sisters at St. Joseph's Villa. Norma and Marion were still there, but my father for reasons only known to him, had taken my older sisters, Margaret and Inez, back. I think he needed cheap labor at his shoe repair shop.

Cheap labor was the reason why he visited me in Norfolk in1942 after not seeing me for eight years. Father then had three shops in Fayetteville, North Carolina and an Army contract to repair boots at Ft. Bragg. He was doing well enough to need an accountant, but cheap enough to want me, a sixteen year old boy, to do it. He offered me a Piper J-3 Cub, and a Plymouth convertible as bribes, but I knew better. When I turned down his offer he abruptly left and I didn't see him for another three years.

We made the trip to Richmond a few days after my eighteenth birthday to visit Norma and Marion. I had always felt guilty about living in a nice house with nice people when my sisters were living in an orphanage run by Catholic Sisters. But they assured me, later in life, that their days at the Villa were the best of their lives.

My orders finally arrived directing me to report to Fort George G. Meade, Maryland on July 7th, 1944, for processing. I was also ordered to report to the local recruiter who issued me a bus ticket, instructed me to only bring a toilet kit, and only the civilian clothes I would be wearing.

The bus departed the evening of July 7th and arrived in Washington D.C. around 2300. Thirty of us then boarded a bus for the trip to Fort Meade. I thought it was an ungodly hour to be arriving anywhere when we were dropped off in front of a warehouse, met by a disgruntled Sergeant who called the roll, then led us inside.

We were issued a mattress, mattress cover, pillow, pillow case, two sheets, and a blanket. We walked two blocks to our new home… an empty barracks. The bunks would arrive in the morning.

The next day was hectic. First, we were issued uniforms, ID cards, and dog tags. We then got shots, filled out reams of paperwork, and were lectured by seemingly disinterested noncoms. We were next informed we'd be leaving by train in a few days headed for Keesler Field in Biloxi, Mississippi to undergo basic training.

The following Sunday we were given open post; so several of us decided to go to D.C. and take in the sights. Having never been further away from home than a hundred and twenty miles, I looked forward to the adventure.

We wore our new khakis and brogans and rode the bus

from the main gate to D.C. where we were shocked to see so many military personnel representing all the branches of the service; most of whom had fruit salad on their chests. We looked like Sad Sacks by comparison, and hoped we wouldn't be noticed.

Catching a cab was impossible, so we walked everywhere, and thanks to our new brogans, we developed blisters on blisters. Thankfully the train ride to Keesler Field took six days, which gave our feet time to heal.

The train consisted of fifteen passenger cars loaded to capacity. The first few days were somewhat comfortable in spite of the humid heat. But the following days were miserable. We spent a whole day side tracked watching an endless procession of freight trains headed north loaded with war material.

No one was allowed to leave the train. The military figured correctly that some of us might just wander off. After six days without bathing, and no change of clothes because our duffel bags were in the baggage car, I'm sure our passenger cars smelled like cattle cars.

We arrived in Biloxi in the morning of the seventh day, and were bussed to Keesler Field arriving around noon. We were dropped off at the largest mess hall I'd ever seen that could seat five hundred men. We were served our first hot meal in a week. I savored every bite, although there were audible grumblings about "this slop." That first day at Keesler we were assigned to flights of forty to fifty men, and then left to ourselves to settle into our quarters.

We met or drill sergeant, Sgt. Albers, who impressed me

as being a strict but fair sort of fellow. He was five feet seven inches and built like a tree stump. His voice sounded like thunder at reveille when he would boom out, "Drop your cocks and grab your socks!" He often punctuated reveille by throwing a fifty gallon drum down the aisle between our bunks.

For the next eight weeks we were subjected to endless hours of drilling, KP, bivouac, rifle training, lectures and the psychomotor tests that would determine who would enter pilot, navigator, or bombardier training. Fortunately I qualified for all three but, of course, I selected pilot training. This brings to mind a training incident that happened the first time I pulled KP duty.

Sgt. Albers picked ten of us to fly the "clipper" the next day. We were to report to the mess hall at 0400. He didn't elaborate further which left us wondering why breakfast was going to be so early. The only "clipper" that came to mind was a large sea plane, the *China Clipper*. Was this to be a special orientation flight for special cadets?

We arrived at the mess hall at 0400 and ate a hearty breakfast. Then for the next sixteen hours, we "flew the clipper" that turned out to be a huge dishwashing machine into which we placed thousands of trays, knives, forks, spoons, and mugs. This was the first, but not the last, time we would fly "the clipper."

Everyone in our flight was a volunteer fresh out of high school who had initially qualified for flight training. Half our flight didn't pass the written or psychomotor tests, and were transferred to other units to be trained as gunners, mechanics, radio operators, or whatever the Air Corps needed. Some fellas expressed their displeasure by going AWOL… and a couple of fellas committed suicide by taking a dive off the water tower.

We completed basic training and were scheduled to undergo pre-flight training at Maxwell Field in Montgomery, Alabama… but the war dictated otherwise. We were divided into pilot, navigator, and bombardier pools and received the designation, 'On the line trainees.' The pilot pool I was assigned to was transferred to the Greenville Army Air Corps base in Mississippi. We would wait there until the need for more pilots arose.

At Greenville, we began training in the Stearman PT-17, a bi-plane with an open cockpit. We then moved on to training in the Vultee BT-13 aka: The Vultee Vibrator, and finally we did our advanced training in the North American AT-6 Texan.

Upon successfully completing all phases of training, we Cadets were commissioned as second lieutenants, or flight officers, and received those coveted wings. The training had taken just over a year and it was looking like the war would be ending before any of us would be in it. But the "Battle of the Bulge" in December of 1944 gave us hope.

We were rousted out of our bunks in the dead of night, ordered to pack, and be ready to ship out on a moment's notice. We were on our way! But, the excited anticipation was short lived. While enroute by train to Montgomery, Alabama our orders were abruptly changed without explanation, and we proceeded to Tyndall Field near Panama City, Florida. We arrived in Panama City early in the evening, then bussed to Tyndall Field where no one seemed to know what to do with us. We were assigned a barracks and informed where the mess hall was.

The next morning a corporal from the orderly room asked us to look around the base to see if there was anything we might like to do. He suggested supply, personnel, the mess halls, flight line maintenance, or even crewing on the base fishing boat. He departed, leaving us to decide what we wanted to do. We thought it was one hell of a way to run a war!

Several of us checked out the flight line, but the fellas there didn't want untrained personnel getting in the way, or tampering with their P-63s and B-24s. Tyndall was a gunnery school where students were taken up in a B-24 to practice firing from the waist position at the incoming P-63s that would make passes at them. The P-63s were modified with heavy armor plates that withstood the frangible bullets that disintegrated on impact. In the cockpit was a counter that scored the hits.

Many of the pilots who flew the P-63s were combat veterans who had seen enough action and resented being fired at; frangible bullets or not. A pilot was actually shot down when a frangible bullet penetrated the space between the propeller spinner and nose of the aircraft. Others had spun in making too tight a turn from the base leg to final approach. A straight in approach with maximum power soon became the norm.

All of us in this job hunting squad had checked out the flight line to no avail. Next stop would be the boat dock where the base fishing boat and rescue craft were berthed

The three rescue craft were used to patrol the gulf whenever there were missions in progress. Many a hapless crew member was pulled out of the gulf moments before he became shark food. We all gratefully accepted an invitation to go on a patrol that lasted eight hours. The craft was similar to a high speed PT boat capable of getting to a downed pilot fast.

Some of our party had never seen a shark, or had ever been fishing. One of the crew took time to teach us landlubbers about the hazards related to a water bailout. When the boat was dead in the water for a while, the crewman started chumming with rancid meat and fish entrails.

I knew sharks would be showing up, having been mostly raised on the Chesapeake Bay. I'd caught many of them, but nothing over five feet long. The other fellas thought garbage was simply being thrown overboard. Within minutes the boat was surrounded by dozens of sharks swimming lazily that were between five and ten feet long.

As if on cue, the sharks went into a terrifying feeding frenzy. The water boiled as they fought for scraps. To make the carnage more interesting, our crewman friend produced a 'grease gun,' (a forty-five caliber machine gun) and fired a few bursts into the boiling water. The sea turned red with shark's blood that attracted even more and larger sharks that began devouring the wounded.
It was sobering for us fledgling pilots to graphically experience this particular water bailout hazard.

To a man we volunteered for whatever job was available. The skipper thanked us for our enthusiastic offer, but informed us he was fully manned and couldn't justify additional personnel... strike two!

We next heard through the grape vine that the Air Corps was still in need of flexible gunners. We discussed the matter of the war ending soon, and our not participating in it as pilots, and all decided to volunteer for gunnery school. But that was shot down... so... I took a job as a helper on the base fishing boat assisting two grumpy civilians contracted to provide fish for the Friday meals in the mess halls.

We fished with a seine approximately one thousand feet long by thirty feet deep. We fished mostly for mullet, and sometimes caught some pompano.

And that's how I finished out the war.

I was discharged in November of 1945 in Richmond, Virginia. With discharge papers in hand, and mustering out money in my pocket, I headed out for Norfolk by bus. I didn't call ahead to my Aunt and Uncle's to tell them when I was arriving because I had no idea myself.

Maggie answered the door when I did arrive, and nearly turned white when she saw me standing there with a duffle bag over my shoulder. She gave me a hug and a warm welcome as only she could as she herded me directly into the kitchen as if I hadn't eaten since she saw me last.
I told her my stories while we waited for my Aunt and Uncle to return from work. She had read all my letters to home and was well informed of my adventures.

A hot shower and a change into some clean civies would

be refreshing, but after the shower, I discovered my Aunt had given most of my clothes to the Salvation Army. What clothes were left, were now too small. I was now five foot seven inches tall and weighed one hundred forty pounds.

Thank God I had my uniforms and fatigues. All GIs were allowed thirty days to get out of uniform. The mustering out money was enough to buy some new clothes, and then some. I also found out that my Aunt had given away my model airplane collection of some 40 specimens; and my baseball card collection! I had some war cards too that came in bubble gum packages; cards depicting the Sino-Japanese War. All given away. Maggie told me when I wrote that I was to be shipped to the European theater soon, my Aunt gave me up for dead and got rid of all the reminders.

My Aunt and Uncle were pleasantly surprised to see me and pleasantly shocked to learn that I had been discharged. We all enjoyed Maggie's fantastic dinner while catching up on the goings on in everyone's lives. My future was a curiosity to everyone... including me.

I told them I planned to enroll at the Virginia Military Institute and eventually enter flight training as an officer, instead of an Aviation Cadet. Surely, in four years, the Air Corps would need replacements for those pilots who elected to return to civilian life. The cost of tuition came up, which was something that I hadn't thought about. I didn't expect my Aunt and Uncle to support me through four years of college, and I had no savings.

My Aunt suggested that I ask my father to sponsor my college education; after all, he then had a chain of shoe repair shops and certainly owed me that much. She further pointed out that he had just returned from Europe aboard the S.S. America and brought back a limousine, and offered, "If he's that flush, surely he could see you through college, especially if you agree to pay him back when you can."

I made the trip to Wilmington to see my father only to be told that he was willing to set me up in my own shoe shop, but he would not give me a penny for college. My sisters were made the same offer but declined. Ole Dad hadn't changed a bit.

In Norfolk I looked up some of my old friends who were now hardened combat veterans. My friend, Jimmy Newby, had been part of the Normandy landing and had been wounded by shrapnel that left one hand useless. He too was thinking about going to college and told me about the G.I. Bill. He also mentioned the 52-20 club that paid an unemployment stipend of twenty dollars a week for fifty-two weeks to discharged servicemen. Millions of service personnel were applying for college; most had been discharged before me. So I was eighteen months in back of the line, according to VMI and William and Mary.

It was no consolation to know that I wasn't the only one without a job. I had little chance of getting into a college anytime soon, and no chance of further flight training. Returning combat veterans were given priority in the job market; even my soda jerk job went to an ex-paratrooper.

The only good news was that the Glenrock Airport was again open for business. I could at least get airborne in a Piper Cub now and then… money permitting. So I saved a little money from my temporary job as a mail carrier during the Christmas season; and there was the 52-20 club.

Most of the fellas who flew at Glenrock Airport were ex-Army Air Corps fighter and bomber pilots who, like me, enjoyed flying the Piper Cub. These guys had flown the likes of the P-51, P-47 and B-24, to name a few. They would have gladly stayed in the Air Corps but Uncle Sam had more than enough peace time pilots. These guys knew I had a paltry number of flying hours, but I was welcomed to the brotherhood as an equal. They introduced me to formation flying, tail chasing, and the verboten… buzzing. It's a wonder why none of us were reported for buzzing; especially the time we flew under the Granby Street Bridge.

On another occasion, a friend of mine wanted to take a picture of me flying low down the Lafayette River. He would be standing on the concrete bulkhead that lined the riverbank. I would pass by him at eye level about twenty-five feet away. The river was straight for two hundred yards, where we chose to take the picture, then made a ninety degree turn to the left.

Directly in line with my flight path was a house standing on a rise that would require me to pull up sharply to avoid it. I wasn't concerned about clearing the house, but I didn't know there would be a man mowing his front lawn with a gas powered mower.

After passing by my photographer friend, I immediately pulled up using full throttle. I banked to the left after clearing the house by fifty feet, looked back, and saw a lawnmower headed for the river with no operator in sight.

I just hoped the mower operator didn't record my buzz numbers. I didn't return to Glenrock until I was practically out of fuel. Luckily for me, all the Cubs were airborne when I landed.

The Glenrock operations fellow informed me that an irate citizen reported a little yellow airplane barnstorming in a reckless manner, threatening life and limb. The operations fellow doubted a novice pilot would do such a thing, but rather suspected one of the ex-fighter jocks was the culprit.

I headed home before any of the other pilots landed; they deduced who was to blame, but never let on. I made a vow to myself that if I got away with this stunt there would be no more buzzing for me! ...of course, I wouldn't be able to keep that vow.

*   *   *

Chapter 3

Northrop and Family

March of 1946 was a very good month for me. I saw the ad Northrop Aeronautical Institute placed in a flying magazine stating they were accepting applications for aeronautical engineering students for classes beginning in June. I sent a request for more information to Northrop in Hawthorne, California, and received their comprehensive brochure describing curriculum and admission requirements ten days later.

The curriculum was math oriented including integral and differential calculus, which was foreign to me. I was comfortable with algebra and trigonometry but I had self-doubts as I mailed off the application papers and my high school transcripts.

I was notified two weeks later that I had been accepted for enrollment under the G.I. Bill, and classes would commence on June 5th...two days before my twentieth birthday. I was advised to arrive a week early to secure accommodations, purchase books, equipment, and deal with all the Veteran Administration red tape.

I boarded a TWA DC-3 for the flight to L.A. the last week of May. Northrop dispatched a van to pick me up along with three other new arrivals. The Northrop staff was cordial, helped us with processing, and finding accommodations. There were no dorms, so off campus rentals had to be found.

I jumped at the chance to move in with four other students who rented a three bedroom house in Manhattan Beach. One of the guys even had a car! We did our own cooking, such as it was, and bought snacks on campus from the "roach coach" that made the rounds to Hawthorne businesses and job sites.

Only veterans were enrolled in the first two classes who were serious about getting an education. There were no fraternity hijinks and class disrupters were not tolerated. There were eight hours of classes daily, five days a week, plus four hours of homework every night, and double that on the weekend. There were no spring breaks, summer vacations, or long Christmas vacation. Socializing was done during the ten minute break between classes, and during the half hour lunch break.

The instructors were all handpicked from Universities and Military Academies throughout America and all were experts in their fields. One instructor had taught engineering at Annapolis for decades before being enticed to Northrop.

Besides the good pay and Southern California climate, the instructors enjoyed teaching students who were serious about learning and succeeding as engineers in the real world. They didn't have to wet nurse and discipline brats whose parents wanted them out of the house… and out of their state.

I did much better academically than I expected by burning the midnight oil and soliciting help from my willing roommates; two who had previous college experience, and the other two who were as bright as new silver dollars. We all got along famously never exchanging a cross word. We cooperated with cooking, cleaning, and shared expenses.

The nearby landlady allowed us to use her washing machine on weekends. Any free weekend time was spent enjoying the sights and sounds of beautiful Southern California. There was no smog back then, the ocean and beaches were clean, there was comparatively little traffic, and the locals were friendly.

Our first excursion was to the Hollywood-Bel Air area to see movie stars. We purchased a map of the stars homes that were all huge and beautiful. We actually saw Clark Gable washing his car in his driveway. He noticed us staring at him, so he flashed that famous smile and waved… which made our day. Sometime later I would see enough stars to fill a galaxy.

My first year at Northrop went smoothly enough. An advantage to attending Northrop was it was situated in the middle of the Northrop Aircraft Corporation complex, making the students privy to tours of the various engineering projects. We could see firsthand how an airplane was designed and constructed.

In fact, much of our curriculum was patterned after techniques and practices Northrop incorporated. This enable Northrop graduates to step right into a design group without going through a trainee period.

In 1946, the students were privileged to witness the first flight of the Northrop XB-35 Flying Wing; a one hundred and five ton bomber designed to achieve maximum efficiency through a radical all wing design. Max Stanley was the pilot and senior Northrop test-pilot.

We also witnessed Howard Hughes testing his gigantic flying boat, *The Spruce Goose*, in Long Beach Harbor. This was only supposed to be a taxi test, but Hughes couldn't resist lifting off the water to a height of about twenty feet. It turned out to be to only time it was ever airborne.

I first met my future wife, Jeanne Drain, in 1947. She was born in L.A., but her family moved to Chicago when she was still an infant. Her family had returned to L.A. in July to purchase a restaurant in Manhattan Beach on the strand next to the pier. And that's where I first laid eyes on Jeanne.

We met during Christmas vacation at her parents White Stop Café where she worked part time when not attending Redondo Beach High School.

She was the cutest being God ever made! She had large, beautiful, soft hazel eyes, the longest lashes I'd ever seen. Her light brown hair was pulled back in a pony tail that fell beneath her shoulders. She only wore enough lipstick to highlight her lips and perfect teeth. She was wearing a green plaid jacket over a turtleneck pullover. After taking my order she turned to disappear into the kitchen, and I then noticed that she was wearing green gabardine slacks and that she was perfect; both front and back!

It took an eternity for her to return from the kitchen with my order. She asked if there would be anything else; so, in well-spaced intervals, I requested jelly, catsup, sugar, cream, and whatever else I could think of to keep her engaged. I was the very type of customer waitresses hate to wait on I'm sure.

When every condiment in the restaurant had been placed in front of me, she left the check and disappeared into the kitchen. Her mother, who I was familiar with from prior visits, came over to chit chat. I abruptly blurted out, "Who in the world is that little 'tootie' that waited on me?" She smiled and asked if I'd like to meet her personally, which was like asking if a bear shits in the woods.

She told me that I'd be welcome to come to their home the following Wednesday at 3:00 pm and she would arrange to have Jeanne there. I accepted of course, but left wondering why I couldn't meet her then and there and why Wednesday at 3:00.

Monday, Tuesday and most of Wednesday dragged on at a snail's pace. I arrived promptly at 3:00 and rang the doorbell. The door opened, and there stood my future bride. She was dressed in blue jeans, rolled up to her knees, a man's shirt, with the tails hanging out, and she was barefoot. I knew Californians were casual and she fit right in. She asked me in and led me to the kitchen where her parents were doing some restaurant related paper work.

When Mrs. Drain saw me, she rose from her chair and said, "Chuck, I'd like for you to meet our daughter Jeanne." The words "our daughter" struck me like a thunderbolt of embarrassment; I had referred to their daughter as a "little tootie" at the restaurant when asking about whom Jeanne was.

Evidently no offence had been taken and we all sat down to get acquainted. Jeanne told me her mother referred to me often as, "the clean cut kid in the overcoat." The Manhattan Beach crowd would never be caught dead in a suit and tie, much less an overcoat. I assured them I only dressed that way for Sunday church.

During our conversations I learned that Jeanne was still in high school. This surprised me because she seemed more mature than a high school kid. I now had two goals in life: one was to become a fighter pilot, and the other was to marry that "little tootie!"

1948 was another good year for me. I was seeing Jeanne regularly; I would graduate from Northrop Aeronautical Institute, and be hired as a draftsman in the control design group at Northrop Aircraft Company. Also, the Aviation Cadet program resumed for qualified applicants with a minimum of two years of college.

Being without wheels, Jeanne and I relied on public transportation whenever we ventured very far. And, Jeanne's brother-in-law, Steve, had a 'woodie' station wagon he sometimes loaned us. In fact, our very first date was in that borrowed woodie.

We went to dinner at Knott's Berry Farm in Anaheim and I remember Jeanne being so nervous and shy that she didn't eat much of what she'd ordered.

In November of 1948, I applied for the Aviation Cadet

program, was informed that my prior enlistment would not apply, and I needed to be evaluated all over again. I at least had the two year of college minimum, and then some.

I put off applying because I needed to build up a bank account by working at Northrop; and because Jeanne and I were discussing marriage. She knew I wanted to fly and would never be happy with a desk job. But neither she, nor I, had any idea of what an Air Force wife would have to endure.

In February of 1949, the Northrop Aircraft Company lost its government contract to produce the XB-35 in favor of the Consolidated B-36 that had a longer range and could carry a heavier bomb load. This changed everything.

Jeanne's Mom and Dad had had enough of the ocean front restaurant business and sold out to Jeanne's older sister Betty, and her husband, Steve. The Drains missed the four seasons, so they moved to Denver, Colorado. They had old friends who had moved there from Chicago who encouraged them to join them.

Jeanne and I talked about getting married after I completed Cadet training. We decided she should go to Denver with her parents while I looked, without success, for a new job in L.A. I soon joined the migration to Denver where, at least, Jeanne and I could be together. I'd play it by ear from there.

There was no demand for Aeronautical Engineers in Denver, so I collected unemployment checks while looking for something else. The Colorado State Highway Department needed draftsmen who could relocate to

Greely, Colorado. The pay was good, for those days, at two hundred and twenty dollars a month. Another separation from Jeanne was out of the question.

With the Drain's blessings we were married on March 30th of 1949, and spent our honeymoon in Greely. Jeanne's older brother, Darrell, made a down payment of twenty five dollars on a 1933 Dodge coupe as a wedding present. I would pay off the balance in three monthly installments. We were now mobile… but our mobility wasn't trouble free.

We packed our clothes and all of our wedding presents that fit in a small box; a pressure cooker, cook book, steam iron, dish towels and a rolling pin. We thought we had it made!

We drove through downtown Denver as a side trip, on the way to Greely, and noticed pedestrians stopping to stare at our car. Of course we thought they were admiring our new old coupe. I rolled down the window to wave at our admirers only to realize that it was the racket that the wooden spokes were making that drew the attention.

Next, as I was shifting gears, the gear shift lever came completely out of the floor! I pulled over and re-attached the lever while wondering what Darrell had against us.

We made it to Greely, which was a very pretty little town where we felt at home. We found the building where I would be working, and began looking for a rental within walking distance. We rented a temporary little one room efficiency apartment containing a hide a bed, a table and four chairs, small stove, refrigerator, a sink, and tiny bathroom. It wasn't much, but we thought it was heaven... for a while.

We moved in and decided to walk the three blocks to the town square to find a nice restaurant. Greely in 1949 was a quiet college town with little to do besides watching movies at either of the two theaters. There were only two cafes to choose from. The beautiful town square had a pond in the center that contained some of the biggest catfish we'd ever seen. The townspeople were very friendly and helpful in giving directions and making suggestions. We chose the suggested café for dinner and ordered just before they closed at dusk.

I reported on time for work Monday morning and was enthusiastically welcomed like a long lost relative. A fellow draftsman and part time disc jockey, who had been there fourteen years, took me under his wing and got me settled in.

He squared me away with a drafting table, instruments, and a drafting manual outlining practices and procedures. This was going to be a piece of cake compared to the projects I encountered at Northrop; including designing a control stick instead of a wheel, or yoke, in the XB-35. As big as the XB-35 was, it handled like a fighter.

Most of my new fellow employees were born and raised in Greely, and few had ventured out of the state. They were fascinated with my stories about the *Spruce Goose*, the XB-35, waving to Clark Gable, and other California adventures.

I felt like a very worldly man about town. Jeanne, on the

contrary, didn't have much to do in our cracker box of a home. She hadn't really made any friends yet, and dared not drive the car anywhere fearing something important would fall off. She whiled away her time by browsing the shops and stores until I came home for lunch or dinner.

We ate out often because Jeanne didn't know much at all about cooking, which was rather ironic. She was raised by a professional chef who had worked at the very prestigious Palmer House and the First National Bank's executive dining room in Chicago. He even owned his own restaurant in Manhattan Beach. After some memorable culinary disasters, she did get better, and then very good in the kitchen.

We'd been married just over a month when Jeanne announced that we were going to be parents. She was elated, but I accepted the news with mixed emotions. We agreed that we were going to raise our own football team, but only when, or if, I eventually completed flight school. I wasn't prepared to be a father on a cadets pay. Anyway… I was happy that Jeanne was happy, and there wasn't any turning back now at any rate.

We were very content in Greely. I was enjoying my low-key predictable job, and Jeanne had become a glowing mother to be. We fell into a comfortable routine that most people would envy. But after several months of this lifestyle, I began to grow anxious about a future that would not include my becoming a pilot. I felt like I was losing sight of my main goal in life. Then I learned the Aviation Cadet program was accepting married applicants. I visited the local recruiting office, filled out the application, and mailed it to Lowry Field in Denver. And began another anxious waiting period.

My enlistment was approved pending the results of the physical. This didn't worry me because I was now five feet seven inches tall, and weighed a solid one hundred and forty pounds. But... that malocclusion condition of mine, which was a non-issue in the past, was now an issue that washed me right out of the program. Now what? After discussing the matter with Jeanne, and a reputable local dentist, I decided to have the problem corrected by dental surgery.

It would involve losing four upper and four lower teeth that would be replaced by permanent bridges for the rest of my life. There was no guarantee that the corrective surgery would even be approved by the Air Force doctors; but it would be worth it if only I could become a fighter pilot. I had to give it a shot.

Jeanne's pregnancy made me doubt that I was doing the right things by undergoing corrective dental surgery, or trying to become a fighter pilot. The families of married cadets weren't even allowed to accompany the cadets to basic training for the first month.

I discussed our predicament, and my feelings, with Jeanne who assured me that a month's separation wouldn't matter in the long run. Where she would stay for the month, and not be alone, did matter. Her parent's place in Denver was tiny, and returning to relatives in L.A. was not appealing.

I suggested that she stay with my sister Margaret, and her husband Max, in Washington D.C. They were good people. I knew Jeanne would like them, and be comfortable with them. They had a big house and a three year old boy who would be a good distraction. My sisters, Inez, Norma and Marion, all lived in D.C. at the time, and would all be supportive as well.

Margaret and Max were all for the plan, so Jeanne and I packed up and moved to D.C. in early December of 1949. I took a temporary job with the Post Office for the Christmas season while waiting for the Air Force to proceed with my application. When the holidays were over I took another job as a draftsman with an aerial surveying company. The pay was extremely good, overtime was encouraged, so money wasn't a big pressure. But I was beginning to think that the Air Force had forgotten me.

Our first impressions of Max left something to be desired. Neither one of us could put our finger on it. There was something about him that gave us the 'willies.' He was cordial enough, but he didn't have much to say about his employment or anything else for that matter. After dinner he would sit for hours listening to operas on their record player. Sometimes he would get our attention by reciting poetry.

After a week or so of living there we decided that Max was weird. Jeanne, nor I, could see what Margaret ever saw in him. My sister, on the other hand, made us feel very much at home and did everything possible to bridge the gap between Max, Jeanne, and Myself.

On February 5th, Jeanne experienced labor pains around 9:00 pm that threw me into a tizzy! It was raining as usual. I called a cab, then grabbed the bag Jeanne had packed a week before. We descended the three flights of stairs and waited in the foyer for what seemed like an hour, even though only 15 minutes had passed. We both ran out of patience and decided to walk the half block to the main thoroughfare where we could easily hail a cab quicker than waiting around. We were successful in immediately hailing a cab and drove across town to the George Washington University Hospital.

Jeanne delivered a boy at 10:26 pm who weighed in at 7 pounds 14 ounces. We named him Charles Wayne Maultsby II, deciding that the II would be better than "Junior." We should have known then that he was destined to become a professional singer and entertainer; you could hear him all over the maternity ward! They even had to isolate him in another room to keep him from keeping all the other babies awake. We find it ironic that he gets paid now days for being loud.

Jeanne and Chuckie returned to Max and Margaret's after three days in the hospital where things got suddenly very uncomfortable for us there. I picked up a magazine that Max left out on the living room coffee table to have a look. I couldn't believe my eyes! It was called, *The Daily Worker,* and wreaked of communist propaganda. It was everything I detested.

Why would he have this trash in his home for everyone to see? I decided not to confront Max with my discovery, but went directly to Margaret. I asked her about the *Daily Worker,* and Max's interest in it. She replied, "Oh, it's just something that Max is into, not seriously. He's always looking for a new cause." My other sisters told me that Max wasn't a "Red", but more like a "Pink." I asked my sisters if Max had been reported to the FBI. They said he had been, the agent told them Max was under surveillance, and that he was only a small fish in a big pond. D.C. was full of "pinkies" in those days.

That did it! We couldn't stay there any longer. How would it look to the Air Force if they found out that I was living under the same roof with a suspected communist? The first thing that occurs upon entering the cadet training program is a security clearance check. One more thing to worry about.

We explained to Margaret that we had decided to move into a place of our own and that we appreciated all that she had done for us. She understood and wished us well, but Max didn't say a thing.

We found a beautiful loft apartment in a private home in Chevy Chase, Maryland that was just what the doctor ordered. It was located quite a ways from my job in Georgetown, but I didn't mind the trolley and bus rides to and from work. And Jeanne was happy.

For the first time she had things to do all day caring for our infant son and housekeeping. She even studied her cookbook more and served some good intentioned efforts. Diapers were cloth and usually hand washed in those days, but the one luxury we could afford was a diaper service.

Chuckie was three weeks old when we decided we all needed an outing. We hadn't seen much of the Nation's Capital at all and decided that Mt. Vernon would be first on the agenda.

We left early on a Saturday morning in our rented car, arrived at Mt. Vernon, and joined a group of about 15 people for the tour. We all moved through each splendidly furnished room where it was so quiet you could hear a pin drop. I was carrying Chuckie, who was on his best behavior, when I noticed him turning red faced and he began to squirm under his coverings. We were just exiting George Washington's bedroom when he let go with a blast that shattered the dignified quiet. Samson would have been proud of such a noise!

The looks I got from the group would have chilled a polar bear. No one would ever believe that the sound they'd just heard had emanated from an infant. It had surely come from the vulgar person holding the infant. Jeanne tried to pretend that she wasn't with me, but the diaper bag gave her away.

* * *

Chapter 4

Pilot Training

Orders finally arrived the latter part of March. My reporting date was the 26th of April, 1950, to Perrin Air Force Base, Sherman, Texas. There I would receive basic flight training in the North American AT-6 Texan, the same aircraft that was used as an advanced trainer during World War Two.

Jeanne and Chuckie would go live with her parents in Denver where they now had an apartment big enough for the four of them. She'd join me after basic training.

Giving my notice at my D.C. job was hard. The entire office crew had been so supportive for the short time that I worked there. The company's president, Mr. Wallace, even informed me that I had been chosen to manage a branch office in Pennsylvania, with a substantial raise in salary if I stayed. I thought about the cadet pay I was going to be receiving, compared to a branch manager's salary, and it made my head spin. I thanked him for the generous offer and explained that I needed to do what I had strived for. He understood and assured me that, if I didn't complete flight training, my job would be waiting for me.

It didn't take long to pack up our footlocker with all of our worldly possessions, plus Chuckie's bassinet, diapers, and other assorted things that babies must have. We decided that, instead of putting out money for train or bus fare, we'd put the money down on a 1940 Ford convertible we had admired in a car lot and drive.

It could have been a smoother trip to Denver. One night we spent at a motel in Salina, Kansas that could have been in the movie, *Psycho*. The burgers and fries I got from the next door diner contained more oil than the Ford's oil pan! That night we turned in early looking forward to an early start in the morning, and arriving in Denver at a decent hour.

Chuckie woke us up around 5:30 am, which was a good thing. Early start, early arrival. Jeanne fed Chuckie his favorite solid, *Gerber's* prunes. We loaded up the Ford having decided to put some distance between us and Salina before breakfast.

Halfway through Kansas, the prunes kicked in and Chuckie started loading his diapers… but good! Jeanne scolded herself for giving him prunes for breakfast and spent the remainder of our trip through Kansas bent over the front seat changing diapers every twenty minutes. She threw the soiled, foul-smelling diapers out the window. There were no roadside litter barrels in those days and we weren't about to wait till arriving at the next town to dispose of Chuckie's 'revenge.'

To make matters worse, we drove into a howling dust storm that lasted two hours before we got out of it. The convertible top on the Ford leaked dust like a sieve.

Jeanne covered Chuckie with a large piece of gauze, but the dust sifted right thought it, leaving him looking like he had been heavily dusted with talcum powder. But he was a stout little trooper and never complained.

Denver was a sight for sore eyes after that 1,650 mile trip across the United States. It took four days of driving, the last day being by far the worst. When we drove up to Jeanne's parent's apartment there must have been five pounds of dust that settled all over the interior of the car. I spent the next day vacuuming and replacing oil, and air filters.

We all received a warm welcome and from there Chuckie received all of the attention. It was the first time the Grandparents had seen him. Grandma took over and gave him a much needed bath before we even unpacked the car. She then clothed him, fed him, and then placed him in his new crib. Jeanne was more than happy to let Grandma Drain look after him after that dog-tiring-long trip.

After settling my new family in with my in-laws, I left Denver on the 24th of April with mixed emotions. First and foremost, it would be four weeks before I'd see Jeanne and little Chuckie again. That is a long time to spend away from a little fella who changes from day to day. Secondly, I was anxious to find out if I could cut the muster, earn the long awaited silver wings, and provide a decent living for my young family. I doubt if there is another woman on earth who would have undergone the trials and tribulations Jeanne endured so I could fulfill my dream.

I laid over in Amarillo, Texas the first night and pressed on for Perrin AFB the next morning. God it was a lonely trip. I kept expecting to look over and see Jeanne sitting next to me holding Chuckie.

When I pulled up to the gate at Perrin AFB, the Ford started making noises like the pistons were changing holes! The Air Policeman asked for my orders and directed me to an orderly room where I would sign in to receive further instructions. He also advised me to park "that thing" before it blew up. I found the orderly room located next to the cadet parking area, leaving the Ford for a well-deserved rest. After all, that car got us to our destinations without any breakdowns. As a lower classman I wouldn't be allowed to drive for the next four weeks.

I was assigned to class 51-C (Fifty One Charlie) along with forty other cadets; half of whom were married. Ours was the next to the last class in which married cadets were accepted. Talk about coming in under the wire! There were six other classes ahead of us in 51-C. A class graduated every six weeks.

It was agonizing to see all the AT-6s lined up on the ramp with no prospect of even getting near one for another four weeks. Our time was spent drilling, physical training, and in ground school learning aerodynamics, navigation, aircraft engineering, Morse code, military law, aircraft recognition, flight planning, meteorology, and communications.

We had to march, or run, everywhere we went. We were always at the mercy of upper-classmen who would stop us, and harass us by asking anyone of a hundred nonsensical questions we were supposed to commit to memory, such as: how many jelly beans does it take to fill the Base water tower? Or, how many rivets are there in the port wing of the AT-6?

Some poor soul, in some class ahead of us, had to actually figure out how many jelly beans and how many rivets. The answers were handed down from class to class, so we didn't have to actually count jelly beans into a gallon jar, or find out how many gallons the water tank held, and multiply the number of jelly beans in a gallon by the number of gallons. And imagine the underclassman that had to count the rivets in the AT-6 wing, who marked each counted rivet with a grease pencil so as not to count a rivet twice, only to have a disgruntled crew chief order him to wash off the entire plane when he was done counting!

Meal time provided little relief from the relentless upperclassmen. There were usually four or five underclassmen assigned to a table that accommodated twelve cadets, the rest being upperclassmen.

A senior cadet sat at the head of the table, and an underclassman, designated 'the gunner', sat at the other end. It was the gunner's duty to see that sufficient food was available and passed around in an expeditious manner. All underclassmen were required to sit on the first six inches of the chair, at rigid attention, looking straight ahead. You could not look down at your plate to place food on it, or to attempt to stab a morsel.

Square meals they were called. Your fork must be raised to mouth level in a straight vertical line, and then horizontally moved to the mouth. If you were lucky there would be food on your fork when it reached its destination.

It seemed to me the cooks were in on the hazing because everything that was served would roll off your fork. I looked forward to the mashed potatoes that would at least stick. I never left the table completely satisfied those first four weeks.

We looked forward to letters from home, so mail call was the only bright moment in an underclassman's day. Jeanne wrote just about every day and sometimes enclosed pictures of Chuckie. He seemed to be growing by leaps and bounds.

Seven cadets in our class resigned during the first four weeks. Some couldn't take the hazing and others realized that the military wasn't for them. In all, thirty one out of seventy six cadets in our class would wash out before completing training. Flying deficiencies accounted for most them, with academics running a close second.

One cadet was eliminated for withholding information concerning his background information. That is exactly why I was nervous about stating I had reason to believe my brother-in-law was affiliated with the Communist party. However, I told it as I saw it and never heard any more on the subject. I received a Top Secret security clearance.

In spite of the hazing, marching, studying, square meals, and sleepless nights for four weeks, those of us that survived could now look forward to our families joining us. And get on with the flying program.

First we had to report to the flight line to be assigned a flight instructor, receive flying gear, including being fitted for a parachute, and collect numerous technical manuals pertaining to operating the AT-6. We were introduced to a "CAPTIVAIR" T-6D that was located just outside our operations building.

The "CAPTIVAIR" was a flyable aircraft that had been placed on jacks and tied down; allowing a cadet to practice all of the procedures necessary to fly the aircraft without ever leaving the ground. The T-6 was a lot more airplane than anything I was used to. The J-3 Cub was a tinker toy in comparison. At first I was overwhelmed by all the instruments, switches and levers, but after many hours in the "CAPTIVAIR," everything fell into place.

Our instructor was 1st/Lt. Russell R. Diment. I liked him immediately. He let us know right from the start that he was there to help us in every way he could, but he would not accept anything but a 100% effort on our part. When we were scheduled to fly he expected us to know all of the procedures. We were to have our local area maps ready and know exactly what we were to accomplish on each sortie.

Sunday was a day off from all the training. Most cadets spent the time with their families, if they were married, or browsing through the towns of Dennison and Sherman. I spent that first Sunday, after my underclassman days, trying to get the Ford started. I anticipated Jeanne and little Chuckie's arrival in the near future. There was nothing that I, or any of my classmates, could do to coax the engine to turnover. I asked a flight line mechanic to have a look and he recommended a complete engine overhaul. I decided an overhaul was out of the question as the cost would be more than the car was worth. It would remain on static display until the finance company finally towed it away.

My first flight in the AT-6, even though it was only an orientation ride with me in the back seat, finally happened on May 15, 1950. Lt. Diment flew me around the local area pointing out the land marks and suitable fields for emergency landings. He told me to just sit back and enjoy the ride. The flight lasted fifty minutes; just long enough for me to start chomping at the bit to get in the front seat the next day. I couldn't wait to call Jeanne in Denver to tell her we were on our way.

Jeanne and Chuckie arrived by bus in Sherman on a Sunday in late May. I picked them up at the bus station in a car that a classmate loaned me. Their trip had been long and exhausting, but Jeanne was grateful that, once again, Chuckie had been a good little traveler.

We checked into a motel until we found a studio apartment in a private home in Dennison. We had to share a bathroom with the owners, but it was affordable on our cadet pay. Married cadets could not live off base, but there was an 'open post' from noon on Saturday until 8:00 pm on Sunday when we could stay with family off base.

This wasn't the best living conditions, but Jeanne assured me that she could put up with anything for a year, and it was better than a year's separation. Chuckie didn't give a damn as long as someone changed his diapers and kept his tummy full.

The transition phase of flying before I soloed was a far cry from the little experience I had in the J-3 Cub. Lt. Diment was a stickler for exact airspeed, heading altitude, power settings, and procedures. He would express his displeasure with any deviation by a grunt into the intercom. I was lucky to have an instructor who only grunted. Other cadets had instructors who would scream and yell from takeoff to landing.

My only complaint, which I kept to myself, was Lt. Diment's habit of lighting up a foul smelling cigar as soon as we departed the traffic pattern. I didn't smoke in those days.

After nineteen hours and fifty-five minutes of take offs, landings, stalls, power on and power off, spins, figure eights, pylon turns, climbing turns, rudder exercises, numerous touch and go landings, on both the Perrin concrete runway and the auxiliary grass field several miles from the Base, the day I awaited finally came.

June 12th, 1950 started out as just another day of touch and go landings at the auxiliary field. I made three touch and goes, was going for a fourth, when Lt. Diment chopped the power and told me to taxi over to the aircraft parked center field that acted as mobile control.

As I taxied over to the mobile control aircraft, I noticed in the rear view mirror that Lt. Diment was unstrapping his shoulder harness and lap belt. I figured that he needed to attend to a nature call… or, I was making him airsick. When I stopped alongside mobile control, Lt. Diment got out of the aircraft with his chute, and began stowing the shoulder harness and lap belt so that they wouldn't interfere with the stick in back. My God, maybe this was it…Solo!

Sure enough, he made his way along the fuselage to the front cockpit and informed me that he would sit out the next few touch and goes. He instructed me that if I encountered any difficulties I was to give him a call on mobile control. I hardly heard a word he said and couldn't wait for him to climb off of the wing.

After shooting three touch and goes Lt. Diment called and asked for a ride back to Perrin. The flight back to Perrin was unusually quiet. I thought that I'd done pretty well; so why was he so noncommittal?

Some of my classmates where there to meet us when we landed and taxied up to the ramp. It was then I learned that Lt. Diment had made a bet with another instructor that his student would be the first to solo. He lost the bet because my good friend, Tommy Mounts, soloed earlier that day. After the debriefing, my classmates bodily carried me to the base pool for the traditional dunking.

Jeanne was just as thrilled to hear the news as I was; but little Chuckie couldn't have cared less. We spent the following Sunday celebrating by eating out and going for a ride in Tommy Mount's car. Tommy was a bachelor from Cottonwood, Arizona. He was a natural born pilot and our paths would cross many times in the future.

From the day I soloed until the end of flight training, the phase of flying I enjoyed the most was aerobatics. Near the end of flight training the instructors would recommend their students for either advanced training in fighters, or multi-engine aircraft.

Lt. Diment took me aside one day and told me he had recommended me for fighters, but there was something I should know before I made my decision. Cadets going on to fighters stood a very great risk of washing out, while those going on to multi-engines had it made because the wash out rate was nil. He added that I could be assured of getting the silver wings in multi engines and then later be checked out in fighters; just to play it safe.

I expressed appreciation for what he was telling me, but told him if I couldn't hack fighters, I didn't want to end up as a co-pilot in a B-36. He then stated, "That's it then, you are going to the fighter school at Williams AFB in Chandler, Arizona."

I completed basic flight training at Perrin on October 18th, 1950, with a total of one hundred thirty one hours and fifty five minutes of flight time in the AT-6. Of the seventy six cadets who entered basic flight training at Perrin, nineteen would go on to advanced jet fighter training at Williams AFB. Our orders read:

> *You are relieved of assignment and duty with the 3555th Training Squadron, Perrin A.F.B. Texas and assigned to Williams A.F.B. Chandler, Arizona. You are to proceed on the 24th of October, 1950 and report no later than the 31st of October, 1950 to your new duty station.*

Jeanne's Grandmother, who was getting along in years and had never been west of the Mississippi river, came to visit and stayed with us our last two months in Dennison. She decided to tag along with us to Arizona, making it four of us on a cadets pay with a thousand mile trip to make.

The government would only pay for my transportation, so a few other cadets and I negotiated a deal with a used car dealership in Dallas to ferry some cars to L.A. for them if they would just pay for gas and oil. We could drop off our families in Chandler; find temporary quarters, and then press on to L.A. The late model Hudson four-door sedan that I was assigned handled our little entourage nicely.

We left Dennison on the 24th of October and made the two-day trip without mishap. We found a motel just outside Chandler near Williams AFB, unpacked the car, fed Chuckie, and then collapsed in a heap.

The next morning I left for L.A., delivered the Hudson, and then hitch hiked back to Chandler where the housing office at Williams AFB was very helpful in finding us a place to live. They recommended an apartment complex named, *Wingfoot Gardens*, where mostly married cadets resided. There were thirty units arranged in a 'U' shape, with a large park-like area in the center. The units were about forty feet by twelve feet with two small bedrooms at one end, a living room, kitchen, and bathroom. This would be home for the next six months… unless I washed out earlier.

Jeanne met and made friends with many of the other cadet wives who all would be good company during the week. Cadet Gus Grissom and family occupied the unit directly across from us. Little did Gus, nor everyone else; know then that one day he would become an astronaut.

"Willie Air Patch" was the popular moniker for Williams AFB that lived up to its reputation for being a no-nonsense, strictly by the book, fighter pilot school. It was a far cry from the comparably relaxed atmosphere of basic flying school. There was a saying, "You didn't have it made until those wings and bars were pinned on you during graduation ceremonies." I saw more than one cadet wash out within a week of graduation. There was no hazing from the upperclassmen, but any infraction of the rules and regulations would make you wish your mother had miscarried.

Most of the flight instructors were veterans of World War II, who served with distinction. They were proud to be fighter pilots and let you know, in no uncertain terms, that you would not get your wings unless they were willing to fly combat with you as their wingman.

51-C was our class and the first class to fly the North American T-28 prior to checking out in the T-33 and the F-80 Shooting Star. The previous classes had flown the AT-6 in advanced flight before going into jets. The T-28 was made for aerobatics. The 800 horse power Wright Cyclone radial engine helped many a cadet out of trouble before it started.

A feature of the T-28, that made landing much easier, was the tricycle landing gear; opposed to the main gear and tail wheel on the T-6 that made it more difficult to land in a cross wind. I saw quite a few 'ground loops' back at Perrin… fortunately, I was not a culprit.

My first flight instructor, who will remain nameless, was one hellova pilot. But he wanted to do anything except instruct cadets. He had to leave a successful charter flight service in Burbank, California when the Korean War called him back to duty. To top that off, he was engaged to a very famous singer, Martha Tilton.

The preponderance of missions in the T-28 was relegated to learning instrument flying under the hood; probably the most boring of assignments a flight instructor could be subjected to. A smattering of formation, aerobatics, and navigation were thrown in, but of the seventy two hours flown in the T-28, most were instrument flights.

My instructor didn't mind the formation phase, but he really came alive when we were scheduled for aerobatic flights. I'll never forget that man as long as I live. He wasn't much for the military bullshit and treated his four cadets as equals. We had enough sense to know that familiarization breeds contempt, but we couldn't help respecting him, while at the same time, feeling sorry for him.

When he briefed me, one on one, for a dual ride, he always asked me for a cigarette. My answer was always the same, "Sorry Sir, I don't smoke." His retort was always, "How in hell do you expect to get through this program if you don't carry cigarettes for your instructor?" I knew that it was his way of pulling my pisser; however, he who laughs last laughs best!

The next time he asked me for a cigarette, I pulled out a pack of Bull Durham, a packet of rolling papers, handed them to him, and suggested that he roll his own. He took the bag and papers and never asked me for another cigarette.

I was scheduled for a range orientation and let down instrument ride. He would brief me as if that was exactly what we were going to do.

Arriving at the aircraft, he would put me under the hood to make an instrument take off. As soon as we were out of the traffic pattern he would wiggle the stick to let me know to come out from under the hood and that he had control of the aircraft. He would then head for an auxiliary air strip named, 'Goodyear,' located several miles from 'Willie Air Patch.' The next hour and a half were spent doing aerobatics off the deck.

We used the air strip as a reference for loops, rolls and landings out of the loop. I enjoyed the hell out of these deviations from the flight syllabus. And who was I to question the behavior and utter disregard my instructor had for turning out a student who could land out of a loop, but couldn't spell the word, *instruments*.

I knew I must pass an instrument check with our flight commander sometime in the near future and assumed that my instructor would get down to business to get me ready. Providence stepped in. I was assigned to another instructor and I never saw, or heard of, my first instructor again.

Captain James C. Hurley was directly responsible for saving my bacon. It only took him ten minutes into our first instrument ride to learn I didn't know my ass from a hole in the ground. He asked how I got such good grades on my previous instrument rides, and what happened to make me forget all that I'd learned. I had no choice but to level with him. He almost made a Hurley size hole in the ceiling when I told him about previous rides. He would have been justified in putting me up for a check ride and washing me out of the program without batting an eye.

Instead, he vented his anger on my first instructor calling him things I never heard of. It's a good thing those two never met. It's a good thing my first instructor had already left for parts unknown.

Captain Hurley made something of a crusade out of getting me past the dreaded instrument check. He even gave up his time off on Saturdays to get me additional instrument rides. Two men were instrumental in helping me get my silver wings; Dr. Varvel, the man who corrected my malocclusion, thus helping me get into the program, and Captain Hurley, for getting me out successfully.

Major Matti gave me my final T-28 instrument check. Major Matti was our flight commander and, thanks to Captain Hurley, I was given a passing grade. I'd like to dwell on the man here because his was a story to be told, and if ever there was an Air Force version of General Patton, Major Matti was it. Even the flight instructors would try to become invisible in his presence.

Not much was known about the Major, other than he came from a wealthy family who owned beaucoup acreage somewhere in Texas. Every weekend he would fly a T-28, or an F-80, to visit his family in Texas. When he returned on Monday morning, no one would get within a city block of him.

Of course, lowly cadets aren't privy to scuttlebutt, but it seems his family had been drilling for much needed water for the ranch for years but were not successful… all they kept hitting was oil gushers. Poor baby; I was taking home $90 a month while he was being cranky about being stuck with another oil well!

An incident occurred, involving Major Matti, during our check out phase in the T-28 proving that what goes around comes around. My flight had been scheduled to shoot touch and go landings at an airfield named 'Rittenhouse.' There was a mobile control unit there where an instructor could monitor the traffic pattern, warn students if their landing gear was not down, their base to final turn was too low, or a myriad of other things a student could screw up.

One day Major Matti was in the mobile unit as an observer when a hapless student entered the traffic pattern and reported his gear down and locked. If the gear is not down and locked a horn will sound and a red light will illuminate to warn the pilot. While the student was making his call, everyone on the same frequency could hear his horn sounding, including Major Matti. The instructor in the mobile unit told the student to, "Take it around, you don't have your gear down." Major Matti grabbed the mike and told the student to land on the next approach and report to mobile control.

I'm sure the student considered heading for Mexico rather than face the wrath of Major Matti in that mobile unit. When we left Rittenhouse and returned to Willie Field, we were lectured for over an hour about numb skulled stunts that can wash you out.

The very next day my flight was again shooting touch and goes at Rittenhouse. I had finished that phase the day before so my instructor, who had mobile duty, asked me to join him and observe the patterns. Everything was going smoothly, until we heard an unfamiliar call sign from an aircraft entering initial for landing. The aircraft pitched out and entered down wind. After rolling out on downwind, the pilot with the unfamiliar call sign, reported gear down and locked, but the gear horn nearly blocked out his transmission. He was told that his gear horn was loud and clear and to break out of traffic and try again.

My instructor mumbled something to the effect that it was a good thing that Major Matti wasn't present or some student would be on his way home. The aircraft broke out of traffic as instructed and called on initial for another try at landing.

This time his traffic pattern was flawless. He touched down and taxied over to mobile control. None other than Major Mattie climbed out of that cockpit and, after a few words about how things were going, he left us to revel in unspoken thoughts. It proved to me that we are all humans capable of doing the unthinkable.

I completed the T-28 flying phase on February 6th, 1951 with a total of seventy two hours. Except for the instrument flying crash course, I enjoyed every minute.

The day before my last ride in the T-28 was Chuckie's first birthday. I wasn't home to help celebrate, but Jeanne made sure he had a festive party with one candle on a cake with ice-cream, shared with invited cadet wives and their small children. Jeanne's Grandmother had returned to Chicago weeks earlier because of failing health.

Up until now we had been flying prop driven training

aircraft, but for the next three months remaining of our flight training, we would be flying the Lockheed T-33 and the F-80 Shooting Star; the T-33 being a two seat version of the F-80.

Prior to our first dual flight in the T-33, each student was given a week's training in a captive F-80 aircraft. We would practice start procedures, emergency procedures, lowering and raising the gear and flaps, and whatever else an instructor would convey over the intercom. Procedures were less complicated in a jet versus a reciprocating engine. As the old saying goes, "Kick the tires and light the fire." That pretty much describes a jet operation.

Jeanne was probably more relieved than I was to see the light at the end of the tunnel with only three months of training left. She never complained about having to make do on a cadets pay. After paying rent, buying groceries and seeing to Chuckie's needs, there was precious little money left for niceties. We envied the cadet families who had cars and received help from home.

I often felt guilty about putting Jeanne through this ordeal. On several occasions I offered that, if she'd had enough, I would resign and return to my job in Georgetown. She would say, "Not another word about resigning, Chuckie and I will see that you get those wings come hell or high water!" With support like that, I couldn't let them down.

Even the single cadets were aware of the sacrifices the cadet wives endured. They knew the wives didn't eat fillet mignon or lobster tails once a week, much less buy a new dress for every occasion.

I don't know how it got started, but all cadets were required to have lunch in the cadet mess hall on Saturdays before leaving for open post. Steak was always on the menu on Saturday. When everyone had been served, the single cadets would get up from the table, as if by signal en masse, leaving their food untouched. The remaining married cadets knew then that the single cadets knew things were not all rosy in *Wingfoot Gardens*.

We gratefully divided the steaks, fruit, bread, etc., and made a lot of wives happy with a full belly. I never heard who instigated this blessed gesture, but I think they deserved two sets of wings, as did everyone who participated.

Another benefactor who did so much to make life easier for some of the cadet wives with children was the man who owned and operated a grocery store across the street from *Wingfoot Gardens*. He knew that, toward the end of the month, some families were pinching pennies and barely getting by. On numerous occasions when he totaled up the bill, he would say, "You can pay me the first of the month if you like." There were more saints than sinners in those days.

I won't go into all the details of every mission during the last phase of flight training in the T-33 and F-80, but I will say it was a heady experience. There was a world of difference between flying a jet and a prop driven aircraft.

After three dual flights in a T-33, Captain Hurley cleared me for solo in an F-80. From then on nothing on earth could shatter my resolve to get those wings… and get them I did!

After sixty four hours and fifty five minutes in the T-33 and F-80; the last flight being on the 26th of April 1951, graduation was now just sixteen days away. If I washed out from this point on it wouldn't be for flying deficiencies or academics. All the ground school had been completed. I could only wash out because of an error in judgment like pinching the commander's wife's fanny or picking my nose in church.

I had seen cadets wash out a week before graduating for a lot less, believe me. "You don't have it made until they pin those wings on your chest and those bars on your shoulders."

I wasn't worried about pinching any fanny except Jeanne's, and I pick my nose in private, so I felt confident that the next sixteen days should go along smoothly. There were uniforms to be tailored, invitations to be sent out, orders to be cut and transportation to my next duty station arranged. Jeanne and I decided to buy my on base roommate's 1948 Pontiac convertible upon graduation.

Every graduating cadet hoped that they would be sent to the Fighter Gunnery School at Nellis AFB near Las Vegas, Nevada. Nellis was rightly called "Home of the Fighter Pilots." Ninety percent of the pilots going on to Nellis would wind up in Korea… Our expectations about being ordered to Korea would be correct, after a short stint in Okinawa and the Philippines for improving flying skills. Classmates such as Childress Clift, being an ex-marine wounded in World War II, were assigned stateside duty.

Only Jeanne's brother, Darrel, arrived to attend the graduation ceremonies. He arrived a week before graduation and shared a bedroom with Chuckie. There were bunk beds in their bedroom; Chuckie always slept on the bottom bunk, out of our fear that he'd fall off the top bunk. Chuckie always felt put out that he couldn't be on the top bunk and expressed displeasure by pointing his little finger upwards and muttering a few unintelligible words.

Things went smoothly in Chuckie's room for a few days, but his resentment of the unwelcome stranger on his top bunk evidently grew to action. Darrel had no idea what was coming and would have moved out in haste if he had.

Jeanne was awakened early on a Saturday morning by a commotion coming from the adjacent bedroom punctuated by every four letter word imaginable. She grabbed her robe and was about to enter Chuckie's bedroom when Darrel bolted from the room dressed only in his white boxer shorts and a t-shirt. He was covered with brown splotches, headed for the bathroom.

Upon entering the bedroom Jeanne was horrified to realize that Chuckie had scooped large amounts of feces from his diaper and had flung it onto the upper bunk, the walls, the ceiling, the floor and of course, all over himself.

Darrel took close to an hour cleaning himself in the bathroom while ignoring Jeanne's pleas to hurry. Jeanne cleaned Chuckie the best she could with soap, water, and a cloth in the kitchen. When Darrel finally came out of the bathroom, he flatly stated there was no way he would ever go near that bedroom again, much less help clean up the mess! Jeanne stripped the beds and endured scrubbing the walls until I arrived home at 1:30 pm... and spent the rest of the day scrubbing that bedroom.

Our orders arrived three days before graduation on May 9th, 1951. We were assigned to the 2353rd Personnel Processing Squadron, Camp Stoneman, California for further assignment to project 2037, 5th Air Force APO 710 c/o Postmaster San Francisco, Calif. We would report to Nellis A.F.B. for temporary duty for the purpose of attending F-80 Combat Crew Training that would last eight weeks. We were to report on May 24th, 1951.

The day that Jeanne and I worked and waited for had finally arrived! The graduation ceremony took place at 10:00 am in the base theater that was packed with friends and relatives. Gen. Spicer and Col. Gray gave short speeches based on, "Every man a tiger." They then administered the oath and began pinning on those cherished wings. Gen. Spicer pinned my wings on while Jeanne pinned the gold bar to my right shoulder and Darrel pinned the other bar on my left shoulder. The ceremony was concluded by another Gen. Spicer speech wishing us god-speed and a safe return from Korea.

It was customary to give the first enlisted man that saluted you a dollar. There were several dozen of them lined up for the occasion as we left the theater.

Afterwards, after I had changed into my new officer's silver-tan uniform, Jeanne, Chuckie, Darrel and I all headed for the Officers Club. The O.C. went all out in helping us celebrate by providing free champagne and food galore… of course club members would see an increase in membership dues the next month.

Chuckie thoroughly enjoyed the party. He received a lot of attention while he enjoyed his finger sandwiches and soda. Jeanne and I had never tasted champagne before and drank the first few glasses as if it were water. I soon felt the effects and suggested that we leave for home while I could still maneuver. Jeanne agreed, but Chuckie threw a tantrum.

I didn't realize that Darrel didn't imbibe or we would have stayed longer. Darrel drove us all home while Chuckie voiced his extreme displeasure… What lung power that little fella had!

Upon arriving home we were surprised by several underclassmen and their wives who were waiting for us to proceed with the party that had started at the Officers Club. The wives had arranged a pot luck dinner and the beer flowed. I changed into Levis and a sweatshirt, but kept those wings that I had waited so long for in my front pocket.

The party broke up at a decent hour and Darrel went to bed, but Jeanne and I stayed up the rest of the night talking about plans for the future. There were many variables to consider in our future including Nellis Gunnery School, Camp Stoneman, overseas assignments, maybe Korea for me… and then what?

We both hoped for assignment to a fighter squadron in Germany. But right now we had to think about vacating our present apartment, a trip to Manhattan Beach for a visit with Betty and Steve, then on to Nellis AFB near Las Vegas to find a place to live. We had twelve days to do it all.

I made arrangements for an Air Force contracted moving company to pack up and move our household. We'll never forget the day a huge 18 wheeler pulled up to our dinky apartment. The semi's trailer was twice as big as our apartment! The driver quickly deduced that he should have brought a much smaller truck after being directed to where all of our possessions were.

We bid farewell to the many friends we'd made who shared the trials and tribulations of cadet life with us, and began our trip to California. We looked forward to seeing Betty and Steve, visiting old friends, spending time with Chuckie together… and just relaxing. For the first time in over two years we didn't have to sweat out making ends meet, and even had a little money left for extras. Jeanne retired the only dress she owned and bought a new wardrobe.

It was less than a day's drive from Chandler to Manhattan Beach so we took our time and stopped sometimes when Chuckie saw something that struck his fancy. We picked the most expensive looking restaurant in Blyth, California for lunch. It was a new experience to order from a menu without looking at the price first. Jeanne reminded me of the times I suggested that I resign from cadets and return to a good job in D.C. We agreed that getting the silver wings was all worth it.

We arrived in Manhattan Beach before dusk and found Betty and Steve's apartment unchanged since we last left it. We were barely out of the car when Betty brushed past us, reached into the back seat, and scooped Chuckie up into her arms, then disappeared into the apartment.

Steve, at least, gave us a proper welcome and helped with the luggage. Betty was sitting on the couch holding and talking to Chuckie when we entered the apartment. She enjoyed teasing me and Jeanne by pretending to take no notice of us... then got up from the couch laughing and assured us that she was equally glad to see us.

We enjoyed three days with Betty and Steve visiting our old haunts along the beach and looking up old friends. We could have stayed longer, but we were anxious to get settled in Las Vegas before I had to report for duty.

I packed the car, Jeanne rounded up Chuckie, we thanked the Shipley's for their hospitality and drove the 285 miles to Las Vegas in six hours.

It was still daylight when we arrived, so we did a little sightseeing while looking out for a motel. The 'Strip' was everything we had heard it was, and then some.

The Flamingo Hotel was the first large casino you saw approaching from the south. We had never seen anything quite like the Strip and were anxious to check it out... but first things first. We chose a motel about halfway between Nellis and Vegas and settled in for the night.

We enjoyed a leisurely breakfast in the motel dining room, and then drove out to Nellis where I signed in at the 3595th Training Group Headquarters to receive orders attaching me to the 3596th Combat Crew Training Squadron. While there, we met a former classmate, Jesse Williams, who was with his wife, Rose, and their son Richard. We all were good friends from our cadet days. Jessie had been attached to another squadron, but we all decided to look for an apartment together and share expenses.

We found a very comfortable, nicely furnished, three bedroom house in an established neighborhood near downtown. Jessie and I would take turns driving to the base so Jeanne and Rose would have wheels for their needs.

I reported to the 96th Squadron on May 27th, 1951, and was pleasantly surprised to find that five other classmates were also assigned there. We all had misgivings about the reception we would receive since we were 'shave tails' fresh out of pilot training. It wasn't long before we were set straight about why we were there and what was expected of us.

All of the instructors were World War II combat veterans who took their job seriously and expected the same from you. We were not looked down upon but rather treated as fighter jocks that were there to learn the skills of the trade.

The better part of the first day was taken up by the phase briefing where we learned what skills we'd be taught. Nellis AFB was known as "The Home of the Fighter Pilots." It was also heralded as the busiest airstrip in the world. From sunup to sun down there was a takeoff and a landing every twenty seconds. I saw as many as six, four ship flights on initial at one time that the tower operators all took in stride.

The dual runways provided the capability of takeoffs from the inside runway, while the outside runway was used for landings. It was not uncommon to hear a pilot call for a flame-out pattern, and have the tower respond, "Roger, you are number three for a flame out pattern."

Something that was condoned, and even encouraged, was the 'bounce.' Anytime you were airborne you were subject to being pursued by another aircraft, or a flight of aircraft, in mock air to air combat. If you saw an aggressor before he got within firing range, 1,000 to 2,000 feet, you could rock your wings to let him know you saw him, but didn't have the fuel or time to engage him. He would then break off the attack to look for someone who could accommodate him.

However, if you didn't see him and he got your tail number, you owed him a beer when you landed.
Our squadron commander was a great one for going up by himself to look for pilots who kept their heads in the cockpit. He usually circled between Nellis and Indian Springs at about 12,000 feet waiting to bounce any single or four ship flight going to, or from, the air-to-ground ranges near Indian Springs. If he managed to sneak up on your wing without being seen, then using an old Air Force expression, "Your ass was grass!" These bounces accounted for the most flame outs.

A fighter pilot is too proud to admit defeat and will continue the rat race long after reaching 'bingo fuel' (bingo fuel is that required to reach your destination with a little reserve) and 'no shit bingo' fuel will probably get you close enough to the field to enter a flame out pattern.

You can understand the environment a fledgling fighter pilot was exposed to forty years ago. Today such training tactics are unheard of… so I wouldn't trade those eight weeks of flying at Nellis for all the F-16s in the inventory today.

I won't go into detail about all the missions we flew, which included formation, navigation instruments, aerobatics, intercept, skip bombing, dive bombing, low angle strafe, high angle strafe, air to air at 12,000 feet, air to air at 20,000 feet, tactical firing on convoy, cross country to another base and return, and actual weather navigation. As our proficiency increased the instructors pushed us further to the edge.

For example… It was during the air-to-ground phase, when we were feeling more like 'hot rocks' than the 'cool stones' we really were, when the instructor tested our mettle.

Whenever he left the gunnery pattern for the flight home, he always badgered us to join up on his wing before he reached a prescribed altitude. He didn't allow for the poor number four man being the last to leave the range, invariably, being the last to rejoin the formation. After several more missions like this we decided to do something about it.

We didn't always fly the same positions on every flight; so on any given day, any one of us could be #4. We decided that none of us would move on his wing until all of us were in position to join up together. Our instructor didn't comment on our little scheme for the next few missions. But he did lay a trap for us later.

We felt pretty cocky about outsmarting an instructor, but we were up against a pro that had ten answers for every question in the book. When he felt it was time to unravel our little scheme he probably stayed up the night before gloating over what we would experience the next day.

It was just another dive bombing and high angle strafe mission that we all could do in our sleep. When #4 called 'bingo fuel' the instructor called, "Last pass and join up." As usual we formed up in a three ship formation and were closing in on the lead ship with pretty good overtake speed, when the lead ship all of a sudden seemed to stop in mid-air! We went shooting by him with speed brakes out and throttle idle. We slowed down to near stall speed when suddenly the lead ship went by us like a rocket! ...Speed brakes in, full throttle and we didn't catch him until he turned onto initial for landing.

During debriefing no mention was made about our embarrassment. We couldn't help but notice the slight smirk on his face the whole time.

It didn't take a Philadelphia lawyer to figure out what happened during the join up and our instructor never confessed. He simply stop cocked the throttle (shut the engine down) causing us to overshoot. Word got around the squadron about the incident, but no one thought much of it other than it was a neat trick… and it showed those 'cool stones' a thing or two.

Hell hath no fury like a fighter pilot scorned and, if it was the last thing any of us did, we were going to get even. Our instructor didn't repeat his stop-cock drill again until we were firing on a towed target at 12.000 feet during the air to air phase of training. On join ups we still performed the same technique of waiting until all were in position before joining on our instructor's wing; and we were wary of overtake speed.

Sure enough, on join up, he stop-cocked the throttle to test if we were on our toes. On a given signal we all stop-cocked our throttles and slid on his wing in perfect formation. He knew immediately what we had done and probably nearly had a heart attack. Here he was, thirty miles from home, responsible for three students with a flame out. None of us had ever made an airstart except in a simulator and if we weren't successful, you could scratch three F-80s.

We could almost hear his heart beat over the radio as he talked us through the airstart procedure. No problem; we all made successful airstarts and returned to Nellis without incident.

From May 28th until July 20th, 1951, I flew eighty sorties in the F-80 to complete the syllabus of training. That's eighty three hours and five minutes of sheer pleasure… and I even got paid for doing it!

While I was having a ball flinging my pink body at the ground, Jeanne and Chuckie, Rose Williams, and some of the other wives took in the sights, culinary delights, and shopping opportunities of Las Vegas.

Sundays were usually spent beating the heat by picnicking atop Mt. Charleston, or swimming at Lake Meade. Boulder City and the dam were a must see along with, of course, The Strip. Jeanne and I were overwhelmed the first time we took in a show at *The Flamingo*. In 1951 there was no cover charge and you weren't badgered into ordering more than one drink. Sometimes we could take in as many as three shows in one night without spending a small fortune.

We felt guilty about leaving Chuckie at the base nursery until we learned he was having a ball organizing the other toddlers and leading them into all sorts of mischief. The poor little fella hadn't had much exposure to children his own age up till then.

All good things must come to an end... So Jeanne and I decided that she and Chuckie would return to California to be near Betty and Steve while I was overseas. She had friends there, she loved the beach and there would be family nearby. So we had yet another trip to look forward to, and settling into another apartment before I had to report to Camp Stoneman.

Exactly where I would be assigned overseas wouldn't be known until I arrived at Camp Stoneman. I was pretty sure it would be Korea, but then, some Nellis graduates ahead of me were being assigned to bases all over the Far East. We stayed with Betty and Steve for only a few days until we found a nice apartment a few blocks from them. I felt better knowing that Jeanne and Chuckie would have dependable relatives nearby.

As the day drew near when I'd have to leave, I reflected back on the life we'd had together since getting married. It was one move after another, living out of suit cases, and now was at least a year's separation staring us in the face. We could not have predicted the Korean War would break out only two months after I entered flight training. After Nellis, had it not been for the war, we probably would have been assigned to a fighter outfit in the U.S., or Europe, where we could be together. It was no consolation that most of my classmates were all in the same boat.

The drive to L.A. International Airport on that early August day to catch the flight to Camp Stoneman, and once again, toward the unknown, was anything but joyous. Chuckie was too young to comprehend what was taking place and probably thought that we were all off on another trip. It would take some time before he started wondering what happened to his Dad. A week, or a year, means nothing to an eighteen month old, so Jeanne would have to explain my absence the best she could.

Saying "goodbye" wasn't part of our vocabularies because it always sounds so final. When the other passengers began to board the plane, we hugged each other without saying a word. I dreaded the moment that I would have to walk away from them, and was the last person to board. I kissed them both, walked out through the doorway, and out to the plane. I can still see Jeanne and Chuckie standing in the terminal as the plane taxied away.

*   *   *

Chapter 5

Okinawa 1951

Camp Stoneman was the processing center for troops going overseas. I learned I'd been assigned to the 26th Fighter Interceptor Squadron ay Naha Air Base in Okinawa. Jeanne was worried that I'd be going to Korea, so I called her with the news. I was joined at Camp Stoneman by one other classmate, Bill Littlefield, but more would follow.

On August 9th, 1951, I departed Travis AFB in California aboard a C-54 for the long trip to Okinawa. It was five days of island hopping all the way; stopping in Hawaii for thirty six hours, then Midway, Wake, Guam and finally Okinawa. Thirty six hours in Honolulu wasn't long enough to take in all the sights. I'd have to see Wheeler Field and the Arizona Memorial some other time; like when I was homeward bound.

Every island still bore the scars of World War II... especially Wake. There were rusting hulks of Japanese freighters, tanks, coastal guns, and numerous fighter planes scattered along the beaches. I tried to imagine what that handful of Marines must have experienced trying to repel the hordes of Japanese soldiers.

We landed at Kadena Air Base on Okinawa on August 14th, and heard that a typhoon was bearing down on the island. Bill Littlefield and I scrounged up a staff car and headed for Naha Air Base and our new assignment at the 26th Fighter Interceptor Squadron. Our arrival timing couldn't have been more perfect…

The squadron was preparing to evacuate all of the F-80s to Japan until the typhoon passed. They were short one pilot and left it up to a coin toss to see who flew; I won.

The next two days were spent getting acquainted with all the members of the squadron who all made us feel at home and welcome right away. Our quarters were Quonset huts that had seen better days. The only permanent building on Naha was the Officers Club.

During World War II, Naha Air Base had been used by the Japanese to launch Kamikaze attacks against the U.S. Fleet. I had the unique experience of meeting a Kamikaze pilot who happened to be a bartender at the Officers Club.

Everyone knows that Kamikaze are one way suicide pilots, but this Kamikaze described himself as the luckiest man on earth. He hadn't been one of those fanatical volunteers who believed that if you died for the Emperor you were assured life everlasting. In fact, non-volunteers were strapped inside a Baka Bomb, not a conventional aircraft, and the canopy was locked from the outside. Once air borne there was nothing to do except try to hit a target. The aircraft was going to blow to smithereens whether it hit a target, land, or sea.

During the U.S. invasion of Okinawa the bartender was

entombed in a Baka Bomb for his final flight. He told me he couldn't get the engine started… and I'll leave it up to the reader to decide if it was a case of couldn't, or wouldn't. He was relieved to become a prisoner of war when he was captured, still locked in his flying coffin on the launch pad, by Army GIs.

While it was customary for a new 'head' reporting into a squadron to get a local area check-out to become acquainted with the traffic patterns, landmarks, etc., I hadn't had much time. The typhoon I mentioned earlier had not changed course making evacuation imperative.

I'm sure the squadron commander, Lt./Col. McCaskill, harbored reservations about taking me along, but he had no choice. Our destination was Iwakuni Air Base, an hour and forty-five minutes away in Japan.

The flight of twelve aircraft was uneventful until we entered the traffic pattern to land at Iwakuni. I was in the last flight of four with two flights ahead of us. The first flight landed ok, but #3 aircraft in the second flight blew tires on landing, causing my flight to delay landing until the runway was cleared.

My flight leader blew tires on landing but managed to clear the runway. Fortunately I had no trouble landing and wasn't required to buy the crew chief, who had to change the tire, a customary beer. Col. McCaskill jibed those who had to buy the beers with, "Perhaps we should let Chuck give us a briefing on short field landings."

That statement couldn't have gone over too well with the old 'heads', but they evidently didn't hold it against me…

They did pull a fast one on me before we left Iwakuni.

Someone suggested that we go to Hiroshima and take a tour to see how reconstruction was going since the A-bomb had been dropped. There were eight of us who changed into our khaki uniforms and set off for what we thought would be a very interesting sight-seeing trip.

We met several Japanese along the way who didn't seem to resent uniformed Americans in spite of the devastation we wrought. Out of politeness they would bow slightly and mutter something in Japanese… until they came to me! If looks could kill I would have had it a hundred times over, but no one in our group seemed to notice. I couldn't understand why I had been singled out as The One who dropped The Bomb on their city until we got back to Iwakuni.

One of the first things Bill and I did, after checking into the squadron, was have the Fifth Air Force patch sewn on the left shoulder of all our uniform shirts. The 'old heads' always kept a 5th A.F. patch-less shirt handy for occasions such as these.

All Japanese had learned to despise the Fifth Air Force, so whoever displayed the patch was less than welcome. So chalk one up for the 'old heads' who must have pulled this stunt dozens of times on unsuspecting 'new heads.' There were disadvantages to being new and there were some advantages. It was an advantage not to be expected to know all there was to know about being a fighter pilot. That comes with the experience of numerous hours in the air. And sometimes a young dog can teach an old dog a new trick.

Prior to our departure from Iwakuni, I had another encounter with a former Japanese World War II pilot. When we arrived at our aircraft, for the flight back to Naha, there was a Japanese man taking his time about refueling my F-80.

He wasn't sure which tank to fill first so I showed him the proper sequence. I sensed he was more interested in the F-80 than he was in the refueling operation. He broke the ice by speaking a little English, and then followed me around with great interest while I made my pre-flight inspection.

He asked me if he could see the cockpit and was amazed when I invited him to climb in. He sat there with his right hand on the stick grip and his left hand on the throttle evidently reminiscing about days gone by.

I asked him if he'd ever flown an airplane; he hesitantly offered that he had been a Zero fighter pilot during the War. I then asked if he had any kills to his credit. Perspiration appeared on his brow and after much clearing of the throat he answered, "Sixteen kills, but they were all Navy, not Army Air Force planes!"

I suppose that he told U.S. Navy pilots he had sixteen Army Air Force kills. I felt no animosity toward this fellow fighter pilot with sixteen kills. He too was just doing his duty as he saw it. My encounter with this friendly man almost made me late for start engines for the flight back to Naha.

We departed Iwakuni on August 21st, flying in weather all the way. We had intended to survey the damage on Okinawa before landing at Naha but the island was socked in. We made a two ship GCA (ground control approach) and taxied to the ramp where Bill greeted us like long lost cousins. He told us about the typhoon and declared his determination not to be left behind again. The next time we would all be left behind.

We sat around the operations building for an hour listening to Bill stories about how he subsisted on C-rations for three days, the ungodly winds that made sleep impossible and the fear that any minute the Quonset hut he called home would be blown off of its concrete pad. Bill was advised by an 'old head' that next time he should ride out the typhoon in the Officers Club, where you'll have hot meals and access to a latrine. The Quonset huts had no plumbing, but there was a community Quonset hut with a latrine and showers… that was impossible to reach in a typhoon. I learned this later the hard way.

I looked forward to mail call most of all because Jeanne wrote almost every day. The letters sometimes backed up in transit, so I'd go without for six days and then get six letters at once. Mostly she described how Chuckie was growing daily and gave details about his expanding vocabulary. Sometimes pictures were enclosed that gave me the right to corner anyone, who would politely have a look, and agree that I had the handsomest son in the world.

The mission of the 26th Fighter Interceptor Squadron was to protect Okinawa from the threat of hostile aircraft based on mainland China. The B-29s stationed at Kadena Air Base, just north of Naha, were flying daily missions over North Korea making themselves a lucrative target. Our squadron sat alert from sunup to sunset, then a squadron of F-82s took over at night. The F-82 was basically two P-51

Mustangs joined by a common wing with a horizontal stabilizer. The pilot sat in one cockpit and the radar operator sat in the other.

Sorties were flown on Combat Air Patrols with at least two armed F-80s in the air at all times and two sitting alert and ready to take off at a moments notice. I had my doubts that the brass really expected a threat from Mainland China, but we were more than willing to meet it head on if it came.

It was during a Combat Air Patrol that I nearly had the chance to shoot down a B-29! Yes, it sounds weird to be shooting down one of your own aircraft, but this one had received extensive battle damage over North Korea and was unable to lower its landing gear. My wingman and I joined up on either bomber wing to survey the damage. We couldn't see any hits anywhere near the nose or main gear doors. The B-29 pilot discussed his problem with the command post at Kadena on the radio and it was decided not to try a belly landing. If the gear could not be extended by any means possible, then the crew was instructed to bail out and the F-80 escort would shoot it down when it was safely out to sea.

The two F-80s sitting alert back at Naha heard the transmission between the B-29 and my flight and offered their assistance. They were as eager as we were to get a little air to air practice in.

My concern was having enough fuel after the crew bailed out, if I didn't, then the alert crew would take off and do the job. The flight engineer on the B-29 managed to mechanically lower the gear just when my wingman called 'bingo fuel.'

We returned to Naha and later learned that the B-29 made a safe landing at Kadena, but because of the extensive damage it would never fly again. This incident influenced the brass to suspend daylight raids over North Korea and confine their sorties to night time only.

Yontan Air Base was an auxiliary field just west of Kadena that we deployed to, five or six crews at a time, to practice air to ground gunnery. The gunnery range was close enough so that we didn't need the wingtip tanks, making the aircraft more maneuverable and capable of sustaining more Gs. We usually spent a week there flying three of four sorties a day. The facilities were skimpy compared to Naha, but everyone looked forward to Yontan.

My turn to deploy to Yontan came on September 3rd, 1951. Low angle strafe, and dive bombing were the order of the day, with no other duties to worry about. All went well until the 8th of September. A day I will never forget.
I was number two in a flight of two taking off at pre-dawn for another gunnery mission. The mission went smoothly until we arrived back at Yontan for landing. On final approach, doing 115 knots airspeed, the aircraft started buffeting, meaning a stall was imminent. I immediately pushed the throttle full forward but a jet engine doesn't accelerate as fast as a conventional engine and I was carrying about fifty percent power at the time.

The right wing dropped and contacted the ground sending the plane cartwheeling while I was repeatedly pitched forward, then sideways, and hit my head hard on the console. I thought that I had bought the farm, but finally the aircraft came to rest right side up. My first reaction was to get the hell out of what was left of the aircraft because of the fire danger.

Luckily the canopy still operated normally so I made a hasty exit to find myself at the bottom of a sixty foot ravine that lined the right side of the runway. I scrambled up the steep ravine, with the fear of an explosion, and fire as a strong motivator.

When I reached the top of the ravine I looked back down to see that the nose, tail, and both wings were gone! I wondered where the crash vehicle was; usually it's at an accident scene in just a few minutes. I waited for what seemed like a long time, then decided to walk to operations.

Soon thereafter the time the crash vehicle appeared in the distance, seemingly in no hurry at all. When it finally arrived the driver got out, without taking much notice of me, and walked over to the edge of the ravine where he stood for a while studying what remained of the F-80. He then took notice of me, walked over to where I was and inquired, "Where's the pilot?" I replied, "I'm the pilot!" To which he replied, "No, I mean the pilot who was in that thing!"

I couldn't convince him that I was the pilot who was in that thing until a squadron mate drove up in a jeep and confirmed that I was indeed the pilot.

The crash vehicle driver was dumbfounded that anyone could have survived the crash, much less climb up the ravine and then stand around as if nothing had happened. He noticed a small scratch on my chin and finally asked if I was ok. I assured him that his services weren't needed.

I climbed into my friend's jeep and left the driver mumbling to himself while shaking his head.

Nobody back at the squadron expected to see me drive up in the jeep, especially the tower operator who saw the whole thing as it happened. He admitted that no one had been in a hurry to pull my remains out of the wreckage. There we no medical facilities at Yonton so a flight surgeon was flown up from Naha to check me out for any injuries. But all for naught as it turned out. Other than feeling numb, after all the thrashing about, there were no broken bones… or so we thought. Many years later it would be discovered that I had broken my back.

The reaction of my squadron buddies were somewhat comical. Some treated me like I was about to have a baby, while others just stood around and stared at me as if I was a ghost. They all expected me to be in a great deal of pain, but my only complaint was that I had missed breakfast and was starved.

An accident investigation team flew up from Naha to examine the crash site and the remains of my F-80. They noted that the canopy had only opened one foot before jamming, which made them curious as to how I'd gotten out of the cockpit with a back-pack parachute strapped on. I had no explanation other than my adrenal glands must have had something to do with it.

They asked me to don a back-pack chute and climb into another F-80 whose canopy was positioned exactly like the canopy on the wrecked cockpit. I could not get out no matter how I tried. One speculation was that I had unstrapped the chute and left it in the cockpit before exiting. But it was secured on my back when I was picked up; so why would I have retrieved it before climbing up the ravine? The only answer was copious amounts of adrenalin at work enabling me to squeeze through the opening in a big hurry.

The investigators noticed yellow paint marks all over the interior of the wrecked cockpit, even under the consoles on either side of the cockpit. Yellow marks were even found in places that were impossible to reach by hand in a sitting position. All the helmets worn by members of the squadron were painted the same yellow color found all over the wrecked cockpit. Only the good Lord knows why my neck wasn't broken.

I flew two more sorties at Yonton before returning to Naha on September 13th. The accident investigation team found the cause of the crash to be pilot error. I couldn't rebut their findings because it was plain and simple; the aircraft stalled and crashed.

Then new evidence appeared when a mechanic discovered wax in the static ports of the air speed indicator systems. Static ports are located flush on the side of the nose section, and all the ports were clogged with wax, causing an erroneous airspeed reading.

Our aircraft were not painted, so they required a periodic coat of wax as a deterrent to salt-air corrosion. Crew chiefs usually were very careful not to wax over the static ports… but someone had. Anyway, the accident board did not reverse its decision and pilot error went into the books as the cause of the crash.

I wrote Jeanne as soon as possible to describe what had happened. It was best that she hear it from me rather than some other source… like a local newspaper article. I enclosed pictures of my wrecked F-80 in the next letter I wrote, and later wished that I hadn't done that. Her seeing the pictures made her fully realize just how dangerous my profession was.

Captain Tom Forcythe was one of the few pilots permanently stationed at Naha allowing for his family to join him. Tom invited me to dinner at his quarters one evening, mostly to prove to his wife that the pilot of the crashed F-80 was alive and well.

She had seen the pictures of the crash site and saw the pieces of the plane loaded on a flatbed trailer. She couldn't be convinced that the pilot, evidently leading a very charmed life, had lived.

 No mention was made of the crash during dinner, but I knew she was dying of curiosity about what went through my mind during and after the accident. Then sure enough, as soon as coffee was served, she began her barrage of questions that went on for two hours.

I enjoyed her enthusiastic, child-like curiosity. She was particularly interested in my reaction when the cockpit finally came to rest at the bottom of the ravine. I described how I was sure I was going to "buy the farm" as the aircraft was cartwheeling toward the ravine.

When the cockpit finally came to rest it was pitch dark, and I felt absolutely nothing. I could hear a hissing noise, but other than that… nothing. My first thought was, "It's not so bad being dead!" Then the pressure on my face required me to push my helmet back off of my face; it had been knocked forward over my face, accounting for the total darkness.

From that point my sole aim was to get as far away from the wreckage as possible. While climbing out of the cockpit I heard myself saying aloud, "Somebody up there likes me!"

Back at Naha it was business as usual flying Combat Air Patrols, instruments, and mock air-to-air combat. I heard later that someone had erected a large sign with bold letters at my crash site that said, **MAULTSBY CANYON.**

I was getting anxious to terminate my stay in Okinawa and get on with the business in Korea. The sooner I got to Korea, the sooner I would be able to join Jeanne and Chuckie stateside.

A tour in Korea consisted of 100 combat missions. Depending on the weather, and availability of aircraft, it was possible to fly 100 missions in about six months. When not flying Combat Air Patrol, there was very little to do on Naha. Bill Littlefield and I did as much sightseeing as we dared, after being warned about things such as unexploded World War II shells, and a commonly encountered poisonous snake called the Habu. Several natives succumbed yearly to the lethal bite of the Habu.

I sometimes saw a small animal, resembling a ferret, wandering around the air field. I learned that it was a non-native mongoose. Prior to the U.S. invasion of Okinawa, during World War II, the top brass were concerned more about casualties inflicted by the Habu than those caused by the Japanese.

To rid the beaches of the snake before landing, a Navy sub surfaced not far from shore and launched several rafts full of mongoose toward shore. A mongoose has razor-sharp teeth and can kill a Habu in seconds with a bite to the back of the head.

A typhoon was headed our way, but the meteorologist predicted it to veer off before hitting Okinawa, leaving us only to deal with strong winds and rain. But he was wrong. The base commander didn't want to evacuate the F-80s unless it was certain that the typhoon would cross the island. He waited too long to decide. The typhoon did not veer off, but came on straight for us with winds over 100mph.

We barely had time to head all the aircraft into the wind and tie them down. Naha was at sea-level, so a tidal surge of several feet could be expected that could wreak havoc on jet aircraft. Saltwater is no friend of aluminum, electrical systems and jet engines. We would pay dearly for not evacuating when we had the chance.

I remembered the advice that an old head had offered about riding out a typhoon in the Officers Club, and intended to do just that. I just barely made it to my quarters to pick up my dop kit and change of clothes when the typhoon hit full force.

I was stuck in my quarters with nothing but C-rations for several days... or so I thought.

There were two other fellas that shared the Quonset hut with me who flew the F-82. We whiled away the first day playing cards, napping and writing letters. There was no latrine in our hut which posed a problem that none of us knew what to do about. By the second day 'mother nature' could be put off no longer; I had to brave the wind and get to the latrine next door. I sure wasn't going to crap in my hat!

I no sooner put my hand on the door knob when someone yelled, "NO!" ...too late. The door flung open like a shot and knocked me back ten feet where I hit the floor with a thud. Debris was flying everywhere when the hut suddenly lifted off the concrete pad about eight feet, then disintegrated into a mass of twisted corrugated sheets of steel. We weren't all decapitated immediately probably because of another intervention from "somebody up there!"

My roommates and I were only dressed in our boxer shorts and t-shirts with shower clogs on our feet. We were far from properly attired for a visit to the Officers Club, about a hundred yards away. We mostly rolled and stumbled to the rear entrance of the OC, that was luckily downwind, and banged on the door until a disbelieving mess attendant let us in. We were soaked to the skin, covered with cuts and scratches, our meager clothing was in tatters, and... we had no club card.

The mess officer came to our aid, provided soap and towels for a shower, and found some mess attendant uniforms for us... but no shoes. We became the laughing stock of the OC occupants who made it a standing joke to order us around like... barefoot mess attendants. I should have just crapped in my hat; after all, I now needed to buy another one anyway.

When the storm abated, we made our way back to where our hut had been hoping to salvage something. All we found was a clean slab devoid of everything except the rusted bolts that once held our home in place. We never recovered any of our possessions or furniture, but some native probably found a windfall.

As I looked around at the devastation it occurred to me that I better get my butt to Korea... where it was safe! Besides, the sea water had reached three feet where the aircraft were parked; it would be a while before we'd fly any sorties. Each aircraft had to be thoroughly inspected and corrosion control maintenance performed.

*   *   *

Chapter 6

BAILOUT/P.O.W.

I got my butt to Korea alright, but, there was nothing safe about it. It was a deadly dangerous place to be.
I was assigned to 35th Squadron of the 8th Fighter-Bomber Group based near Sumon, Korea at the Fifth Air Force's K-13 advanced airfield. It was an outfit that had seen nothing but constantly rugged combat in the thick of the Korean War.

I had successfully completed sixteen missions of the "dirty" kind; shooting up trains, roads, and canals and hitting enemy troops with napalm, rockets, guns and bombs on close support missions. And anything else that might be necessary in the grim ground-support tactical missions of the Korean air fighting.

The seventeenth mission promised to be mean and costly. The strike was against a concentration of armored vehicles, tanks, supply trucks, and troop reinforcements at Kunri in North Korea, a rail and road center of critical importance to the Communists. It would be well defended; every pilot expected that.

Taking off in pairs, our squadron of F-80 Shooting Star fighter-bombers lifted sluggishly from the runway. Each plane carried a 1,000 pound bomb beneath each wing. Takeoff in the F-80 with a full load of fuel, ammunition, and the ton of bombs is a long dragging affair.

The airplane responds poorly to the controls. To correct the problem of takeoff you had to roll in a lot of nose-up trim. Immediately after becoming airborne, you'd roll the trim back to hold the nose down and accelerate to a safe maneuvering speed.

As I rolled the trim back for a nose-down pressure, a circuit breaker suddenly popped out. The trim became instantly inoperative. After my vehement cursing of the damn breaker I had to make a quick decision. To fly all the way to Kunuri would now require me to push hard on that stick all the way to the target and in the glide bomb runs; and twice as hard on the way back to K-13 after the fighter had dropped much of its weight. My arm would be numb upon landing.

Although no one would blame me if I turned back, I decided to stay in formation and fight the stick all the way there and back. My previous sixteen missions taught me the value to our ground-pounders of the deadly load I carried in bombs and machine-gun bullets. What the hell; fighting trim is a lot better than lying in a foxhole with poor ground- pounders. It was the least I could do.

Of course we could not have anticipated what would happen that day. Nobody knew that Kunuri was a trap. The Chinese brought in dozens of light and heavy guns, including several batteries of deadly, accurate 88-mm. flak guns. They realized Kunuri was too lucrative a target to pass by and that the fighter-bombers would be coming. So they augmented the bait with a bristling wall of flak guns.

I sure as hell didn't know this, and neither did I know the circuit breaker that popped out so annoyingly would literally mean the difference between life and death. Or that the very trap the Chinese had set up at Kunuri would also save my life. Fate takes strange turns with pilots and few men will know so bizarre a chain of circumstances which allowed me to suffer impossible odds... yet survive.

When we reached and circle the target, we were stunned at the fury and volume of the anti-aircraft pouring up from the ground. Great clouds of oily black smoke, their centers marked with blotches of angry red, erupted everywhere in the sky. Tracers hosed in broken lines from the hidden guns. "We'll never get through that stuff with glide-bombing!" a pilot shouted. The squadron leader agreed and ordered us to change the attack to dive-bombing. And at this point the series of miraculous incidents began. Death tried hard several times to snatch at me, but fortunately, miraculously, without success.

I rolled over almost on my back, and shoved the F-80 into a steep dive. Suddenly, at an angle of sixty degrees, a heavy shell crashed into the side of the airplane and the world blew up in my face. At the moment of the explosion I was concentrating all of my attention on the rail lines with their freight cars packed with supplies when all hell broke loose; a fantastic shock smashed through the airplane and slapped me with a giant hand against the side of the canopy.

The shell exploded just about seven feet behind the cockpit. The blast ripped forward into the throttle quadrant, dissolved the instrument panel, and transformed the windscreen into a blur of cracked glass.

Sharp thuds slammed into the back of the seat; the armor plating saved my life, stopping a barrage of jagged shards of metal.

At the same instant a flash fire whipped through the cockpit. I looked down to see my left arm wrapped completely in flames. I stuck my left arm straight out into the air where the windblast snuffed out the fire.
And that was when I realized through the numbing shock of the explosion what I had done. I had extended my arm to the side *into the air!*

This is where the first intervention of fate paid its dividend. In the glide-bombing attack I would have flown with my hand on the throttle, on the left side of the cockpit. The decision to dive-bomb is the only reason why I have a left arm today. When the shell hit the bird it blew out the whole side of the airplane, throttle quadrant and all.

Because of the dive mission, my hand was at that moment on the gun sight right up forward, just above the instrument panel. I was changing the depression of the sight. In glide-bombing you need more depression on the sight to predict the bomb fall; dive-bombing however, is virtually line of sight.

Several things happed almost simultaneously. When stuck my arm out into the airstream, extinguishing the fire on my blazing arm, the move was not made intentionally because of the fire. The blast had knocked out the F-80 control system, and I immediately knew I couldn't control the aircraft. The stick was useless and moved about without response from the fighter. I was diving straight in to the earth, helpless, out of control. I had just seconds to live.

But remember that circuit breaker that popped out? The trim controls were inoperative, and I had been flying with a stiff forward pressure on the stick the whole time. Because of the jammed trim causing a steep nose-up position, the moment the elevator controls were knocked out, the airplane responded to the trim and pitched up with a violent jerk. My hand went out into the airstream because I had reached for the throttle.

I knew at once that I had to get out of the airplane. I was going to tell the guys that my controls were shot out, that I had no elevator response. I reached out for the throttle quadrant to press the radio switch and, of course, nothing was there, just a tremendous hole. The whole side of the airplane had been blown away!

After a period of time, training becomes instinct, as does training specifically for emergency situations. When the stick failed to respond, without even thinking of the motion I squeezed the bomb release and a ton of metal and high explosives fell away from the airplane toward the target. It is this sudden release of weight combined with the nose-high trim that caused the tremendous pitch up of the F-80. All this happened within seconds. The jammed trim control had saved my life by preventing the wild dive into the ground. But the succor was only temporary.

The Shooting Star pitched up, and unless I got out fast, the airplane would continue in its wild zoom and tumble crazily out of control. I may not be able to get out!

A fleeting thought came to me. "No use sitting here any longer" Later, I was amazed at the calmness of that thought, because at that same moment I was in critical danger. The pitch up was so severe that violent g-forces rammed my head down between my knees. My legs were straight out and I couldn't lift my head; I had no throttle with which to chop the speed of the fighter. I grasped the ejection handles and yanked back hard. As I pulled to actuate the explosive charge, I instantly remembered that this is the way a pilot loses both legs, chopped crudely off at the knees by their being smashed into the front of the upper canopy. It was not a pleasant thought, but I had no choice.

Call it what you will, another miracle perhaps, but as the seat exploded with ram rod force out of the airplane, it tumbled forward. It is impossible, it cannot happen, but the tumble caused my legs to miss the sharp canopy edge- perhaps by no more than a thousandth of an inch!

There was a terrific roar when the airstream struck my ears. The sky and the horizon tumbled crazily before my eyes. There was no automatic separation device from the seat. I was at low altitude. I thrashed my legs, the legs that should have been severed, and kicked the seat away from my tumbling body. The pilot chute snapped away dragging the canopy out in a long streamer and then CRAA-CK! In that moment the tumbling flight ended and I was suspended beneath the blossomed silk.

It should have been quiet; other pilots have described the sensation of drifting earthward beneath the silk. It is no more than a quiet sighing of the wind. But not then.

There was a terrifying din; a tremendous, constant crackling roar in the sky. Three squadrons of jet fighters screamed earthward, engines howling. A forest of heavy anti-aircraft guns and cannon blasted away in an upward hail of fire. Bombs smashed into the earth, the concussion waves rippling out and slapped at my body.

The earth was covered with heavy white snow. I floated down beneath a chute that was all white; had it been red and white the other pilots would have seen me, and know that I had ejected safely. But my parachute canopy and the snow blended into one; I was invisible.

I floated gently to earth… directly into the center of the target. At the same time a half a dozen thousand-pound bombs struck the ground, and found myself in the middle of a violent, blazing hell of explosions and waves of concussion.

I hate to say it, but it's a good thing those guys couldn't hit what they were aiming at, because they sure as hell would have killed me. On the way down I thought the Chinese were shooting at me. The chute was riddles with holes and I could even hear the bullets passing right by my ears. But they weren't; they were just firing madly with every gun they had at the planes.

Once on the ground, I slipped out of the parachute harness and dashed madly away from the target center. A knoll in the distance became my objective.

Get behind the knoll, away from the firing, disappear from sight and run for it while the Chinese were focusing all their attention on the sky.

I made it away from dead center of the target, but failed to get very far. I was much closer to the knoll when two thousand-pound bombs exploded less than a hundred yards away churning the earth into a vibrating volcano of flame, shock, and thunder.

A fist slammed me against the ground. I was dazed and disoriented when I gained my feet and started running again. But there were twelve airplanes in their dives and the bombs continued to smash into the earth. Every time I got to my feet and ran, the shock waves hurled me heavily against the ground again. I was knocked down a half dozen times in my attempt to escape capture. But I only managed to cover only a few hundred yards when suddenly I found myself facing a ring of rifle muzzles held by Chinese soldiers... and all pointing unerringly at me.

I was listed as Missing In Action (MIA). Not one of my fellow F-80 pilots saw me parachute to earth. However, they did see the blazing fighter that I had recently been in whip crazily through the air, then explode as it hit. No one believed I was alive after those events of 5 January 1952.

It's probably difficult for anyone else to decide what was worse: my harrowing experiences in the air and my incredible brush with death, or what I endured for the next twenty-two months as a prisoner of the Communists.

When the Chinese captured me, I didn't see a friendly face for many weeks afterward.

My captors kept me isolated from any American or other Allied prisoners. Not until I was brought to an interrogation room at Anju did I meet another POW. This was a B-26 pilot shot down on a low level attack; his presence was a great joy to me.

We stayed together for the next several months, living in a prison cave dug into the side of a hill. The cave was not quite high enough for a man to stand, or to lie with feet outstretched. We slept and lived on filthy straw, passed our body wastes almost like animals and endured all the discomfort, and sometimes the horror, of living in a stinking hole in the ground infested with all manner of insect life and rodents. It was bitter cold. And for all those months we subsisted on rice and some water… nothing else. After once complaining about being fed nothing more than a plain bowl of rice a day; were told that our Chinese guards received nothing more or less.

During those trying months we never relented in our attempts to escape. Atop the cave was a strong, but crude structure of boards. My hole mate and I tried every way imaginable to dig, scrape, or gouge our way out of there. Our efforts were intense and unremitting, but success was not to be had.

The remaining time at the hands of the Chinese, and sometimes with the North Koreans, began to melt into a blur of unreality. There was pain, intense pain. The months filled more and more with hunger and privation, with cold, and with interrogations that went on endlessly.

It is really impossible to describe what took place day after day, week after week, month after month.

I cannot, and neither can anyone else, condense into the pages of an entire book the terrible psychological impact of those two years. It is impossible to assimilate because there are too many aspects to digest; there are no bridges of eloquence to convey the utter loneliness at times while enduring the sharp, penetrating scalpel of the Chinese methods of psychological torture.

Pain and torture was an everyday occurrence to those people. To us it is horrible, starkly horrible. Yet much of that same torture, torture of everyday living is intense only by the contrast of comparison. They often treated their own people the same way as us. You come to understand this; you *must* understand the enormous, yawning gulf that creates the variance of thinking, of psychology, or you begin to bend. And you can bend only so far; you must have resilience, belief in yourself, in your country, in what we were doing over there in those stinking caves and prisons. If you believe, you can stand *anything.*

Exactly what happened to me is a story that must stay locked within my own memories. I'll leave it to someone else to tell their story of pain and keeping insanity at bay… day in and day out not ever knowing what day it was. Suffice to say that I was dragged and shoved and prodded from place to place, rarely knowing where I and my fellow prisoners were.

There was solitary confinement. When I refused to co-operate with the Chinese; they resorted to beatings. I resisted interrogation and made it clear that I was an enemy of the People's Republic… solitary, beatings, starvation. I tried to escape, which was unthinkable to the Chinese, and because they did not care very much for the lives of their own fellows, I came very close to being shot or skewered by irate Chinese guards with long bayonets.

Never once did I yield. I bent only so far, but that was all. To yield, to break, was more than to receive the assurance of an end to the maddening physical and psychological treatment. To yield, even to claims so ridiculous as to be impossible to believe, was to be false to everything that I believed in, that I loved. To me there were never two choices. It was as simple as that.

One bright moment came in the darkness of the twenty-two months. Beginning an interrogation in a closed room, a Chinese officer spoke to me in perfect, crisp English. He noted my raised eyebrows and waved his hand casually. "Relax Lieutenant Maultsby," he said. "This will not be the interrogation you expected." He offered a cigarette. I accepted it and breathed deeply, gratefully of the smoke.

The Chinese officer explained his command of the language; he had received his education at the City College of New York. He did not press me at all with questions and explained that he had left the United States only to visit with his family still in China and was then trapped by the outbreak of war in Korea... and the commitment of Chinese forces to the battle.

I spoke frankly. "You're an educated man. You've lived in the States, obviously you know us well. My God, do you really believe all this Communist nonsense?"
The Chinese smiled and shook his head. "Of course not, you have answered the question yourself."

Suddenly his hand slapped the table. "But what can I do?"

He almost shouted. "My family is in China. Nothing would be more satisfying than to walk over to your lines, to return to the States. But no, that is impossible. If I were to make that mistake they would wipe out my family to the last person; my immediate family and every relative they could identify…"

He fell silent and pushed the cigarettes across the desk. An hour later he informed me that I would have to return to the prisoner compound. But before I left, the Chinese rose to his feet and said quietly, "Good luck."

I needed every bit of that luck. There were more interrogators and a repetition of everything I would like to wipe from my mind. But time passed, the guns were stilled. On September 1st, 1953, I was in an exchange of prisoners.

Despite the privations of the two years as a prisoner, and the loss of forty-five pounds, the doctors told me that I was in surprisingly good physical shape. Your physical shape depended a lot on your mental shape. If you wanted to be convinced that you were in a bad way, that's just how a man usually ended up. Too many men, good men in all other respects, wallowed in self-pity, or gave up hope altogether. And that broke them.

If you believe in what you have been taught are the important things in life, in honor, morality and country; if you believe in these things with all your soul; then they can never get through to you. You can take anything.

*   *   *

Korean Bailout addendum:

One of the things Jeanne told me made the hairs rise on the back of my neck...

The night before she received the horrifying telegram listing me as missing action, little Chuckie woke up screaming, "My Daddy, My Daddy, My Daddy!"

Jeanne rushed into his bedroom to find him sitting up in his crib, wringing wet with perspiration. She tried, but there was nothing she could do to console him. He kept screaming, "My Daddy, My Daddy!" for another five minutes. Then, as suddenly as his screaming had started... he stopped. He lie back down and fell fast asleep.

Jeanne stood by his crib overcome by a horrible premonition thinking, "Something has happened to Chuck... I just know it!"

The next day, around one o'clock in the afternoon, a young woman arrived at the house to deliver what Jeanne feared was imminent. The young woman asked if she could come in and was directed to a couch where she and Jeanne both sat down.

The young woman fidgeted for a few moments before producing the M.I.A. telegram. She read it to Jeanne who felt herself grow numb with shock. The young woman then asked if there was anyone Jeanne wished to be notified. Jeanne asked her to notify her Mom and Dad. Also her sister Betty, and Steve, who came to the apartment immediately to be with her.

Korean time is seventeen hours ahead of California time. The time of my bailout and Chuckie's nightmare were in sync.

Chapter 7

How to Become a Thunderbird

We wanted at least a week off to get settled after arriving at Nellis AFB before I had to sign in on November 20th, 1953... which was Jeanne's birthday. There were no vacancies in Wherry housing, so we rented a house in the Huntridge subdivision near downtown Las Vegas. Our furniture and personal belongings arrived the same day we did so we didn't have to live out of a suitcase in a motel again.

It was the first real home either of us had lived in for quite some time; Jeanne had a ball getting things organized. Chuckie pitched in and helped get his room in order. He was proud of his maple bunk beds and matching dresser. He couldn't understand why we wouldn't let him sleep on the top bunk... until a few years later.

It was a heady experience not having to pinch pennies anymore. If Jeanne wanted an accent piece for an end table, or whatever, she went right over to the Ethan Allen store and bought it. She especially enjoyed setting a fancy table with Noritake china. She had a service for twelve, until Chuckie accidently reduced it to a service for eight, requiring the use of plastic plates and glasses from then on.

I was pleasantly surprised to learn that Jeanne had learned a lot about cooking from her father while I was gone for two years.

I signed in to the 3595th Flying Training Wing on November 20th, 1953, and was assigned to the 3594th Squadron. I was amazed at the reception I received from every member of the squadron. There were five other ex-POWs assigned to Nellis.

There were nothing but hundreds of F-86s on the flight line; along with a few T-33s and B-26s that were used for towing aerial targets. I couldn't wait to get into the cockpit of an F-86, but I knew I would need to check out in the T-33 and build up some flying time first. You needed to successfully complete an IP course of instruction and several hundred hours in the aircraft before you could become an instructor pilot in the F-86. I didn't mind flying the T-33, or even a Piper Cub, at that time.

Several of my cadet classmates, who had completed one hundred missions in Korea, had chosen Nellis for their next assignment. Our class suffered heavy casualties in Korea. I was saddened to hear of several cadet classmates who didn't make it back.

The day after I was assigned to the 3594th Squadron I flew two missions towing targets in a T-33. On the first mission I rode in the back seat, then flew the front seat on the second mission. They didn't waste any time getting me back in the harness and after two more rides in the T-33, I was on my own. I was fully checked out.

The next F-86 Instructor Pilot class wasn't scheduled until

January 11th, 1954, so I had to content myself with towing targets in a T-33. It was routine, except for one incident, when a student pilot pressed in too close at a low angle off. In spite of my warning to break it off, he pressed in and shot my right tip tank off! His flight was making right hand patterns so he had to have noticed my T-33 in his gun sight as he was firing.

And sure enough, his gun camera film showed him tracking the target at zero angle off with the pipper traversing from my left wing tip, through the fuselage, onto the right tip. If there is such a thing as a guardian angel, mine is number one.

I was asked to sit in on the flight debriefing once we landed. The flight leader shot down five Mig 15s in Korea making him an Ace. He had no tolerance for a breach of air discipline and chewed on that poor student's ass until there was nothing left. There was nothing I could add except, "Don't do it again!" That gun camera film was shown to every student during their initial aerial gunnery phase briefing for years after.

Christmas 1953 was my first since 1950. I was home with Jeanne and Chuckie doing what I liked best… and that was flying. As if Chuckie wasn't spoiled enough already, I bought him a *Lionel* electric train set. I always wanted a *Lionel* electric train set, so Chuckie had to want one too… right?

While shopping for the train, Jeanne asked Chuckie what he wanted Santa to bring him. He immediately answered, "A little brother!" He couldn't have known that we had been working on a little brother since I arrived back home.

During the weeks before Christmas I'd wait for Chuckie to go to bed, so I could set up the train in the kitchen with the door closed just to make sure everything worked. The smoke pellets worked so well that they were used up, except for the few that Jeanne hid from me, by Christmas morning. And on that morning at 7:00, Chuckie burst into the living room and made a bee line for a little plastic car under the tree. He never noticed the train. So, I finally got the *Lionel* electric train set I always wanted.

On January 11th, 1954, I was scheduled to attend the F-86 Instructor Pilot School on base. I was the only one in class who hadn't flown an F-86; everyone else flew one in Korea. I arrived thirty minutes prior to the flight briefing and noticed that I was scheduled to fly #3 in a flight of four with 1st/Lt. Chips Carpenter as the flight leader. I hadn't even read the dash-one (an F-86 operating hand book), attended ground school, or flown in the F-86 simulator, so there must be a mistake!

Chips showed up five minutes before five o'clock briefing dressed in civilian attire and feeling no pain. When I told him that I'd never flown an F-86 he didn't even bat an eye. He told the rest of the flight to take off singly and do aerobatics or whatever. He changed into his flying suit and said he would give me a supervised start and chase me in another F-86 (there were no dual cockpit F-86s). He went over a few emergency procedures on our way out to the flight line and told me to just give a call if I had a problem. Chips was a natural born fighter pilot who I'd flown with on numerous missions back on Okinawa.

The flight went well; the F-86 was everything I expected and more. It handled like a thoroughbred without a mean bone in its body.

My next flight was solo, without a chase pilot, and remains the quickest check out in a different aircraft I ever experienced. Not having the required number of hours in the F-86 to complete the IP course, I was sent back to my squadron where I alternated flying tow missions in the T-33 and flights in the F-86. This went on until March 1st, when I became an IP in the F-86.

There were numerous pilots at Nellis who had Mig 15 kills to their credit and there were a dozen aces. But most of the fellas in the squadron were more interested in hearing about my experiences as a POW. Between flights I would be bombarded with questions until my flight commander, who was an Ace, had enough. He approached me and declared, "You know Maultsby… it doesn't take any skill to become a POW." What he said was true, but why he said it left me speechless. He later became a POW in Vietnam for six years.

Speaking of POWs… Eddie More paid us a visit while on a cross country. I'd lost touch with him and I wondered why his wife didn't meet the ship when we arrived back from Korea. He described how his wife was standing in the middle of the living room when he arrived home in San Diego and announced, "I want a divorce." What a homecoming! Poor Eddie hadn't gained a pound since I last saw him in spite of a good appetite.

There were several bachelors in the squadron who visited the Maultsby household frequently. Doug Brenner, in particular, stopped by every Wednesday night to watch Bishop Fulton Sheen on TV. He always arrived after dinner with a six pack of beer and a bag of chips. "Hi Charlie" or "Hi Jeanne" was his usual greeting to whomever answered the door. Doug had an identical twin brother, a naval aviator who, with the help of his brother, once played a good prank on us.

One Wednesday night, Doug's brother Dave showed up at the front door with beer and chips in hand. I invited him in and mentioned that he was a little late to which he replied, "No sweat Charlie, I had a little car trouble." Dave played with Chuckie until it was his bedtime and wasn't interested in Bishop Sheen.

The doorbell rang and Jeanne nearly fainted when she opened the door to see Doug standing there. He said, "Hi Jeanne," and walked in with a shit eating grin on his face, fully aware of the dumbfounded looks on our faces. Their mannerisms, voice and looks were identical; making it impossible to tell them apart. Doug and Dave had a good laugh and I'm sure this wasn't the first time they ever pulled that stunt.

Dave once showed up at the squadron wearing his Navy uniform. Our squadron commander, Lt. Col. John Hancock, saw him and sternly demanded, "What the hell are you doing wearing THAT outfit?"…Before Dave could answer, Doug appeared, causing Col. Hancock's mouth to fall open as he looked from one to the other in disbelief. From then on, no one was ever sure if we were in the presence of Doug or Dave. Doug went on to fly the right wing position with the USAF Air Demonstration Team, the *Thunderbirds*.

I thoroughly enjoyed instructing all phases of fighter gunnery to pilots fresh out of flying school. There were some instructors who avoided the initial check out phase like the plague. They didn't relish flying wing on a student who had never flown an F-86.

You had to herd the student from takeoff to landing through every maneuver including stalls, aerobatics, touch and go landings, spin recoveries and whatever else the syllabus called for. I built up a lot of time in the F-86 in a short time. I was always available to take a flight whenever another instructor begged off. Though no instructor ever gave up a gunnery mission.

During the summer of 1954 we moved on base to Wherry housing and I got a motor scooter to get around on. Chuckie was going to get a belated Christmas gift in the form of a baby brother, or sister; so now Jeanne wouldn't have far to go to the base hospital for checkups and had the car at her disposal. The doctor predicted the baby would arrive near Jeanne's birthday. It seemed that all of our friends and neighbors were having babies… or planned to, which prompted a bachelor, Captain 'Nifty' McCrystal, to rename Wherry Housing to "Weary Hosing."

Nifty was a legend around Nellis… and Las Vegas. He was the only bachelor on base whose house was always open to students and instructors alike. He referred to everyone as "nose picker." But no one took offence.

He spoke in a whisper that was uncharacteristic of a gregarious fighter pilot. There were usually half a dozen, or more, students and instructors at Nifty's house for happy hour. But Nifty would never drink martinis if he was flying in the morning and took a dim view of anyone who did drink and flew in the morning. There were occasions when flights had to be cancelled because students and instructors spent too much time at Nifty's, or on the Strip and were in no condition to fly a jet aircraft. It's true that you can always tell a fighter pilot, but you can't tell him much!

Nifty had a girlfriend back east. He once decided to take her a gift of a goldfish in a bowl by hopping in an F-86 with the fishbowl riding on his lap. He encountered a severe thunderstorm near El Paso that whipped his aircraft around like a leaf, causing him to use up fuel and dumped the fishbowl contents in his lap. Being low on fuel, he decided to 'drop in' unannounced on Biggs AF**B,** almost directly under him. You do not 'drop in' unannounced on a S.A.C. base. Biggs AFB was the home of a B-36 Wing with the highest security. Nevertheless, Nifty landed and was about to turn off the runway onto a taxiway when a weapons carrier appeared pointing a 50 caliber machine gun directly at him.

Before opening the canopy he removed his helmet and placed the fishbowl over his head. Soon his aircraft was surrounded by more weapons carriers and several staff cars. He opened the canopy and announced, "I come in peace from another planet!"

Of course none of the S.A.C. types saw any humor in any of this. The Wing Commander gave him one hour to get his ass off his base with orders never to return again.

Once a year our squadron participated in a joint Air Defense exercise conducted by the Western Air Defense

Force based seven miles north of San Rafael, California at Hamilton AFB. We never knew when an exercise was coming, so we all kept a 'bug out' bag packed and stored in the personal equipment room with the parachutes and helmets. These exercises always occurred on weekends to avoid disrupting the flight training schedule.

When the 'balloon went up' (jargon for attack imminent), we dropped everything and prepared for deployment to Hamilton. We deployed in flights of four, refueled upon arrival, and then waited for notice to scramble for a possible intercept of an enemy bomber. We wouldn't know if it would be an exercise, or the real thing, but our guns were fully armed.

We were briefed if an enemy bomber got past the Farallon Islands, that are fifty miles off the California coast, and we didn't make an intercept with the 50 calibers; then we should consider ramming the bomber in a head on pass.

There was little hope of missing a bomber with the 50 calibers, then doing a 180 degree turn and catching it before it reached San Francisco. Ramming wasn't a pleasant thing to consider, but if you considered how many lives you could save by doing it, it made sense. Hopefully the intercept would be made before the Farallons and we wouldn't need to resort to Kamikaze duty.

This occasion was an exercise where we made many intercepts on target aircraft. We gained confidence in the radar directors who gave us vectors to the targets and their range. All intercepts were one hundred or more miles off the coast.

Every time I took off from Hamilton AFB, I'd take a good look at the Golden Gate Bridge and the nearby wharf where the *General Black,* the troop transport that brought us home from Korea, docked just a year ago. I remember taking a picture of the bridge when the *General Black* was directly beneath it as we entered the San Francisco Bay.

We were usually scrambled in pairs for an intercept. On my last intercept mission I was leading the two ship element and decided to do a little sightseeing after we completed the mission. My wingman wanted to shoot a few GCAs (ground control approaches) before he made his final landing. I told approach control I was going VFR (visual flight rules) and my wingman would stay under their control.

I started a letdown about twenty miles off the coast and felt drawn to the Golden Gate as if it were a magnet. My better judgment told me not to even consider doing it… but I did it anyway! I passed under the bridge at 350 knots and immediately felt better for having gotten that out of my system. Then the worry about consequences began. Was I observed on radar? What was the penalty for such a stunt? Anyway, when I returned to Hamilton, no one mentioned anything and I never heard a word about it.

Jeanne's birthday, November 20th, came and went, but the little bundle we were expecting didn't arrive until November 30th, 1954. The bundle turned out to be a red headed little boy weighing seven pounds eight ounces. We named him Shawn Brandon Maultsby. We marveled at the red hair, until the doctor offered that my 'pipes' were probably just rusty. Chuckie no longer believed in Santa Clause, but thanked us anyway for providing him with a brother. He was as proud as a peacock and couldn't wait to show off his new brother to all his friends. He insisted on being the one to carry Shawn into the house when we got home from the hospital and placed him on a platform rocker in the living room. Shawn still has that very rocker today, although it's been re-upholstered a few times.

I was promoted to Captain and made a flight commander on February 23rd, 1955. A few months later, our squadron received the first F-100 Super Sabers in the Air Force which I checked out in on June 24th. But before I go on, I'll tell one more F-86 story…

The 3525th Squadron had a research and development detachment manned by some of the brightest minds in the fighter business. Major Latshaw developed an improvement for the F-86 A4 radar ranging gun sight. It was called the Delta Dot system, but I really don't remember what it was. Anyway, he wanted to have two IPs from another squadron, who had no knowledge at all about the new system, come down to fly several air to air missions so he could evaluate the results. My friend and neighbor, Herb Bloschies, and I were chosen for the honor. The new system was a winner that helped me and Herb double our scores.

There were other countries, which had the F-86, who shared our interest in the new development. Dignitaries from all over the free world were constant visitors. After my last mission, using the Delta Dot system, I was walking through the hall of the 25th Squadron headed for Major Latshaw's office; absentmindedly trying to dislodge a stubborn booger. Just as I reached his office, and turned to enter, I ran headlong into the biggest man I'd ever seen exiting the office.

I still had my finger up my nose when he extended his huge hand for me to shake. I quickly removed my finger from my nose and I could feel the booger dislodge and it now was sticking to my finger. I quickly hit my hand on my 'G' suit in an attempt to wipe it off before I took the man's hand in mine.

After shaking his hand I could have died from embarrassment! With his hand still extended he said, "I say old Chap, I believe this is yours!" He indicated, with a fixed stare, where the booger was on his hand and waited patiently while I fumbled through my 'G' suit searching for a handkerchief. After I removed the troublesome booger, he walked on after cheerfully saying, "Cheerio!"

The big man was followed by our wing commander, General Roberts, and several other generals I didn't recognize. I knew the big man was some kind of high ranking officer because of his highly decorated uniform. Maybe in the R.A.F., or something, judging by his accent.

He turned out to be the Chief of Staff of the Royal Australian Air Force!

After we were debriefed by Major Latshaw, he thanked us for flying the missions and shook Herb's hand. He didn't offer to shake mine.

The next morning I received a call from General Robert's secretary ordering me to report to his office immediately! My heart sank knowing what was coming. I was there in less time than it takes to tell… while dreading every step.

The secretary motioned me directly into the general's office where he was sitting at his desk with his arms folded and his head down so low that I couldn't see his face. I hit a brace, saluted and said, "Sir, Captain Maultsby reporting as ordered."

He sat immobile for what seemed like a very long time and then finally said, without looking up or returning my salute, "Maultsby… You just don't go around wiping boogers on visiting dignitaries, especially dignitaries like the Chief of Staff of the Royal Australian Air Force!" I stuttered. "Yes Sir!" …then, "No Sir!"

He excused me with a, "That will be all." I did an about face and hauled ass out of there! I had serious doubts, before I entered his office, that I would have an ass when I left… And Nifty was right. Everyone is a nose picker.

Back to the F-100 Super Sonics… Where Doug Brenner was selected to be the first pilot in the squadron to check out in it. He flew out to Edwards AFB, California, where a North American Aviation Company test pilot briefed him for thirty minutes and assured Doug that he would be in the tower if there was any trouble.

There were no technical manuals, so it was simply up to Doug to light the fire and see what happens. He had never flown an aircraft with an afterburner and stated that it was the biggest thrill of that first flight. He flew several more sorties at Edwards before bringing the first F-100 to Nellis, where he busied himself with getting the rest of us checked out so we could go ferry more F-100s from the North American plant in L.A. back to Nellis.

It was a thrill to fly an aircraft that had less than an hour and a half flight time, and soon we had twelve brand new aircraft on the flight line.

I looked forward to going supersonic, straight and level in the beast, but was disappointed when I did. There wasn't any sensation what-so-ever. Unlike the F-86 that could exceed the speed of sound in a vertical dive, all sorts of things happened letting you know that you had broken the sound barrier.

First you had to split S from 45,000 feet diving straight down at full power. As the airspeed built up you encountered buffeting as the aircraft tried to push through the wall of air built up in front of it called compressibility. The instruments go berserk and the control stick reverses; that is, if you pull back on the stick, the nose drops and vice versa. Once you punch through the barrier, everything returns to normal. During the recovery from the dive, as airspeed decreases, the same sensations are experienced passing through the subsonic barrier.

The other squadrons envied our not having any students to worry about, but that abruptly changed. As soon as we built up enough time in the F-100 to be considered combat ready and IP qualified, everybody at the Pentagon came to Nellis to get a flight in a supersonic aircraft.

The generals came first, then the Colonels and Senators. Senator Goldwater and Senator Cannon, both reserve Air Force generals, came to receive a checkout. We had less trouble with Goldwater and Cannon than some others who were only suited to flying a desk.

There was initially no dual cockpit F-100s, so we had to chase our charges in another F-100. We resented having to spend as much time with one individual as we would have with a class of thirty students.

Hours of briefings, simulator rides and blindfold cockpit checks were required. Just so they could go back to Washington to place a model on their desk and a certificate on their wall stating they had broken the sound barrier. I think most of them would have refused a second flight if it had been offered.

Eventually we started welcoming students right out of pilot training who had been checked out in the F-100 in other squadrons at Nellis.

In April of 1956, I attended the Squadron Officers School (SOS) at Maxwell Field in Montgomery, Alabama. The school lasted sixteen weeks, which was a long time to be away from the F-100. It was Jeanne's first experience in the Deep South and she was unpleasantly amazed by the segregation policies that were prevalent in those days. Several other officers attended SOS the same time I did who also brought their families.

Wally and Didi Carson was a childless couple who was there and had an apartment next door to us. Didi often asked Jeanne if she could watch Shawn at her place. Jeanne was, of course, happy to be relieved of a rambunctious eighteen month old for a while. Shawn hadn't uttered his first word yet, so Didi took it upon Herself to, at least, teach him to say Mama or Papa.

After working with him for days, she finally lost her

patience, and said, "shit" in anger. Shawn looked at her and very plainly repeated the word "shit." That was his first word… and the end of Didi's grammar lessons.

I had accrued some leave time so, after graduation from SOS, we drove up to Norfolk to visit my Aunt and Uncle to show off our second born.

Of course they made a big fuss over Shawn and the first morning there my Aunt picked him up and asked him what he wanted for breakfast. He replied, "shit"… she almost dropped him in shock and demanded of Jeanne, "What have you been feeding this Child?" I'd never seen Uncle Louie laugh so hard and Shawn became his favorite right then and there.

After a week visit in Norfolk, we began the trip back to Las Vegas in our 1955 Buick station wagon. The first day out was a rainy Sunday afternoon. We were miles from any sizeable West Virginia town when all hell broke loose in the rear end of the Buick! Parts and piece of the differential were scattered all over the highway. The only sign of civilization was a house about a mile ahead.

Luckily it was a downhill coast to the house where, believe it or not, a man greeted us who happened to be the chief mechanic at the local Buick dealership.

He knew all about the trouble 1955 Buick rear ends were having because of the recall to modify the differentials. We were invited to make ourselves at home while he collected the pieces and made the necessary repairs that took only an hour. He assured us we'd make it home and advised us to go to the Buick dealership in Vegas to have the proper modification to the differential completed. He said that we didn't owe him a cent for his service and sent us on our way.

Several miles down the road Jeanne looked over at me and said, "You know something, you really do have a guardian angel." ...I was beginning to actually think so too. We made it home safely, but not without constantly worrying about the rear end self-destructing again.

For the remainder of 1956, until March of 1957, I made up for all the time I lost in the F-100 by going to SOS and Norfolk. I felt more at home in the cockpit than I did in my easy chair and made three or four sorties a day the norm. That March I was selected to attend the Fighter Weapons Instructor Course conducted by the 3525th Squadron there at Nellis. Graduates of the course were considered to have the equivalent of a PhD in fighter pilotage.

Half of the day would be spent flying and the other half in academics for ten weeks. After completing the course I was sure that I would get an overseas assignment, preferably Germany. I wanted Jeanne and the boys to see Europe and experience the things that some of our friends and neighbors had told us about. Some of those friends had left three years earlier and had returned to find us still there. Surely 1958 would be my year for an overseas assignment.

In February 1958, I got orders alright… I left the squadron to become the Air Operations Officer with the Standardization and Evaluation Board at Group Headquarters. Assignment to 'Stand Board' was an honor, but I would rather have gone to Europe. The upside was that I was now in a position to fly as many sorties as I pleased; without having to conduct phase briefings, flight briefings and debriefings, sessions in the simulator, or making out the schedule for the next day's flying.

Every instructor pilot at Nellis had to undergo a proficiency check flight once a year, plus a no notice flight check conducted by Stand Board. The six of us on the Stand Board were kept busy.

We received the next day's flying schedules from the five squadrons and decided who needed a no-notice, or proficiency check, based on our records. If it were to be a scheduled proficiency check, the instructor would know of it days in advance and put on a good dog and pony show. The instructor would be aware of a no-notice check only when a Stand Board member would show for the pre-flight briefing in flying gear and take the #4 man's place in the flight.

We evaluated the instructor on the way he conducted the briefing, the flight, the debriefing and adherence to IAW rules and regulations too numerous to mention. We stressed safety and air discipline until it came out their ears. General George S. Patton once said, "All human beings have an innate resistance to obedience. Discipline removes this resistance and by constant repetition, makes obedience habitual and unconscious."

Being the 'Supreme Court' of the flying program kept us on our toes. We had to keep up with all the changes in the numerous rules and regulations and see to it that the squadrons were so notified. We seldom wrote up an instructor for failing to conduct a briefing or flight in a professional manner. After all, Nellis had the cream of the crop in the fighter business… just ask any one of the pilots!

Captain Cal Davey was a member of the Stand Board who had several Mig kills in Korea and was a two time member of the Nellis gunnery team that won the 1954 and 1956 worldwide gunnery meets. Squadrons from around the free world would send their top guns to Nellis every two years to compete in every facet of fighter gunnery. Some said that the home strip had a lot to do with the Nellis teams winning every event. And some of the other team members forgot why they were there and played too hard on the Strip in Las Vegas.

In June of 1958, Col. Bruce Hinton, our group commander, and a Mig killer in Korea, chose Cal to be the operations officer for the gunnery team that would compete in the October, 1958 meet named "William Tell." If anyone knew how to manage a gunnery team, it was Cal. He was charged with the responsibility of selecting eleven instructor pilots from Nellis who were considered top guns. These eleven would participate in a shoot-off to see which four would comprise the Nellis team with Col. Hinton as the leader.

It was during Cal's selection process when he yelled across our operations room and asked, "Hey Mosby, how about trying out for the team? I'm making up a list now!" Cal always called me Mosby, and later the "Grey Ghost," a reference to John Singleton Mosby, the Confederate cavalry battalion commander during the Civil War. I answered, "No way! There are assignments overseas in the mail and I'm past due for mine!"

Two days later I received the list of pilots that had been selected for the shoot-off. My name was amongst them. I accepted the news with mixed emotions because any pilot would give anything to be selected, but I wasn't sure how Jeanne would like the idea. The heat and sand storms in Las Vegas were getting to her. But she accepted the news as she always did saying, "You know you want to do it, so what's a few more months?"

Col. Hinton flew with us on every flight and took notes of our scores in all the events that would be part of William Tell. The competition was fierce and when Col. Hinton called us all into his office to announce the team, he started off by saying, "I'd be proud to have all of you on my team, but there is only room for four." Then he read off the four names; Major Jack Brown, Captain Dean Pogreba, Captain Waymond Nutt and Captain Chuck Maultsby.

My heart skipped several beats when he mentioned my name, because frankly, I didn't expect to be selected. The meet was scheduled for late October, which was when new assignments would be announced. I said to Cal, "Now look what you got me in to!" Cal replied, "No sweat Mosby. If you guys win the meet, you'll get your choice of assignment." Well now, that was more like it, and what an incentive to win the meet.

Jeanne was thrilled to hear that there would be a choice of assignment if we won the meet. Of course, she had no doubt that we would win. But a new wrinkle cast doubts amongst the Lone Tigers. The Lone Tigers being our team's adopted name.

Nellis AFB was, and had always been, part of the Air

Training Command (ATC). All of the other teams were comprised from Tactical Air Command (TAC) Wings throughout the world. Some general decided that it was time for some team, other than Nellis, to win a meet.

When Col. Hinton learned that we had to use the F-100F (a dual cockpit F-100) instead of the F-100A, I could imagine what went through his mind. Not that the F-100F wasn't a fine airplane, it's just that it was used mostly to check out new pilots and for giving instrument checks. The gun sights and ordinance delivery systems just went along for the ride and I'm sure some had never been actuated. Also, ATC wasn't as supportive as usual, citing budget problems, etc. So, if that's the way they were going to play the game, then we became determined to have the last laugh.

Col. Hinton assigned each of us an airplane and assembled the finest maintenance crews available. Sure enough, there were numerous glitches in the ordinance delivery systems that took weeks to correct. There was one benefit the higher-up general provided without knowing it.

It was sometimes difficult for a pilot to describe a glitch in a system plain enough for a maintenance man to understand the problem. With the dual cockpit F-100F, we could take the maintenance crewman along for a ride to see for himself what the problem was. Usually the crewman would know what the solution was before we landed, saving many hours of trouble shooting.

I can't say enough about the dedication and professionalism of the maintenance personnel who worked grueling hours, around the clock, to make sure we had the best gunnery platform available. The ordinance personnel took our aircraft out every night to the harmonization range to fire our guns, making sure they were always zeroed in. With support like that, there was no way we were going to let them down. During periodic and 100 hour maintenance inspections, they worked literally all night to make sure we would have an aircraft to fly the next day.

It was policy that no one but the aircraft commander would fly his airplane. If his aircraft was out for maintenance, he didn't fly. I never missed a flight because of my aircraft being grounded. Thanks to ATC, there were no spare aircraft assigned to the team, which made me believe they were in cahoots with the rest of the Air Force to make sure we didn't win the meet. But win it we did! And I couldn't help but gloat over the fact that all the other teams had all the support that money could buy.

We often shot perfect scores while winning every event on the agenda. We had watched the other teams arrive for the meet in their brightly painted aircraft, and flashy flight suits, while we flew aircraft with a checkered tail and wore comparatively drab orange flight suits.

We wore a patch depicting a tiger sitting in the cockpit of an F-100 with the words, LONE TIGERS, below the F-100. The Lone Tigers sure showed the Air Force what a determined bunch of people could do in spite of the odds against them.

The Air Force Chief of Staff, General Curtis Lemay, presented Col. Hinton with the William Tell trophy, along with trophies for every event we won.

Just prior to the meet, Nellis was incorporated into TAC, but we had to represent ATC for the meet giving credence to the old saying, "If you can't beat 'em, join 'em."

After a lot of celebrating, we all came back down to earth and contemplated what was next. Cal said we could pick our next assignment if we won the meet. Jeanne was thrilled with the thought of going to Bitburg, Germany for the next three years and I wanted her to be happy.

There was no one around at Gunnery Team operations the day after the meet when I stopped by to clear out my locker. But in walked Major Robby Robinson, the leader of the *Thunderbirds*. He dropped by to ask if any of the Gunnery Team members would be interested in trying out for a position on his team. The right wing man on the Thunderbird team, Captain Sam Johnson, had completed his two year tour so the position was open. Robby asked me to ask around for him. I assured him that I gladly would.

That evening I told Jeanne what Robby had told me. She could tell I was chomping at the bit to try out with the *Thunderbirds*, which would mean another four years in the heat and sandstorms of Las Vegas.

The next day I mentioned to Brown, Pogreba and Nutt what Robby had offered, but none of them were interested. That evening when I mentioned to Jeanne that there were no takers for Robby's offer she said without hesitation, "Oh yes there is, go for it! You know damn well that you'd give both of your testicles to join the team." I pointed out that it would mean another two years in Vegas and she said, "Just go try out, it doesn't mean that you'll be selected."

The next day I called Major Robinson and informed him that I was the only Gunnery Team member interested in trying out for the 'T' Birds. He said, "Fine, be down here tomorrow and we'll do a practice show."

I showed up at the appointed time, Robby briefed me on the show sequence we would be doing and asked if I had ever done any formation aerobatics. I answered that I hadn't other than following students through their aerobatics at a respectable distance.

The briefing was short, so I had time to talk to the other T-bird pilots before going out to the aircraft. Homer Whitlow, Gayle Williams, Sam Johnson, Fish Salmon and Herm Griffin gave me a crash course on what to expect, and they were all adamant about one thing, "Whatever you do, don't fall off his wing!"

The take-off and flight to Thunderbird Lake, a dry lake bed thirty miles north of Nellis where the Thunderbirds practiced, was normal. Once there Robby called, "Trim 'em up!"

While straight and level, he attained a certain airspeed, while we trimmed the aircraft for hands off flight. For the next twenty-five minutes I was subjected to the most grueling flight I had ever experienced. When Robby was satisfied that our wings were overlapped by three feet, he pulled up into a five 'G' climb to perform a whifferdill. When we were vertical, headed straight up, he quarter rolled to the left and pulled through until we were upside down. As our noses fell through the horizon, he did another quarter roll to the left, until we came out opposite of the direction that we began the maneuver. As soon as we bottomed out of that maneuver, pulling five Gs, he pulled up into a loop maintaining the same Gs. And when we bottomed out of the loop, he pulled up into a barrel roll.

By this time my right arm was killing me! Being subjected to four, five and six Gs without a let-up can be considered attempted murder!

Horsing a 28,800 pound monster around the sky was work and Robby wasn't finished with me yet. We did several more rolls, loops, and a 360 degree vertical turn that was gut wrenching, to say the least. I was never so happy to call 'bingo fuel' than I was that day. The flight back to Nellis gave me a chance to shake out my right arm, but he never let me vary from the three foot wing overlap until we pitched out for landing.

Robby didn't say a word on the return flight to Nellis, nor did he say anything to me when we gathered at T-bird ops. He went directly to his office and left me wondering.

The other pilots asked me how it went and I admitted it was a grueling workout that left me soaked with perspiration. I hung around for another thirty minutes expecting Robby to debrief me on the flight, but he didn't come out of his office. I finally went home for a much needed rest.

Captain Chuck 'Fish' Salmon, who flew the slot position with the T-birds, lived directly across the street from us in Wherry Housing. He dropped by our house early that evening to ask about how things went. I told him I hadn't gotten the word and then I asked him how many other pilots were trying out. He answered, "None so far." He offered that as long as I maintained position on Robby's wing, a little bobbing wasn't anything to worry about.

When Jeanne asked me how I thought I did, I couldn't come up with a good answer. Flying with the T-birds is something the average fighter jock would never experience and I considered myself an average fighter jock. I could at least tell our grandchildren I actually got to fly one time in a red, white and blue Thunderbird airplane.

I then took a long hot soak in the tub to help relax my tensed muscles. Following that was one of Jeanne's superbly cooked dinners.

The next morning, as I was about to leave home for my duties at the Stand Board office, I got a call from Fish Salmon. He told me that Robby wanted to know why I hadn't showed up for work at T-bird ops yet. I'd heard that Major Robinson was a man of few words, but this was ridiculous! He never said a word to me after the tryout flight, so how the hell was I supposed to know I'd made it without other pilots even trying out yet?

Of course I hustled right down to T-bird ops and was greeted with much laughter and congratulations. Everyone knew I had made the team. Even Fish knew when he came over to the house last evening. This was all just their way of pulling my pisser. Even Robby managed a big grin. Not in a million years would I have ever expected that I would achieve the ultimate honor of becoming a Thunderbird; especially during the struggles of my cadet days.

The first time I saw the Thunderbirds perform was at the SOS graduation exercises in 1956. They were flying the F-84 Thunderchief then and both Jeanne and I marveled at how four pilots could attain such flying proficiency. She had asked back then, "Would you like to do that someday?" I answered simply, "Fat chance!"

Normally the new team member would take over as the solo pilot, while the solo pilot would move up to the diamond. But Herm Griffin was happy in the solo position, so Robby approved my replacing Sam Johnson as the right wingman in the diamond. It would be ludicrous of me to write much about the *Thunderbirds*, because that has already been done by Martin Caidin, a brilliant aviation writer. Martin already had beaucoup books published and more than a thousand magazine articles before he spent six weeks flying with the team in 1960 gathering material for his book, *"THUNDERBIRDS."*

I'll never forget meeting Martin at our annual show at the Daytona Raceway in Daytona Beach, Florida. I was in my motel room, trying to take a nap, when the door burst open and in walked Dick Crane, the T-bird narrator, followed by a human dynamo. Dick introduced me to Martin and announced that he would be spending the next six weeks with us. I had no idea it had been arranged for him to join us and write a book about his experience with us. We hit it off immediately because of his almost uncontrollable love of flying. I remarked to Dick, "Now we have our own Bookie."

Jeanne remembers her first meeting Martin at Nellis, when Helen Crane brought him over to our house one afternoon while I was down at T-bird ops. She described him as a "whirling dervish," who never sat down for even a moment.

As he and Helen were leaving, he spun around and announced, "By the way Jeanne, I'm working on my first novel that's going to take place in Mexico!" When Jeanne asked if he had a title yet he responded, "Yeah! All Flies Are Spanish." ... and he was gone in a flash.

We later had Martin over for a very enjoyable dinner and evening. Of course, the conversation the whole time was all about flying. Jeanne had purchased one of Martin's books titled, *"The Night Hamburg Died"*, out of curiosity about the man. She read it cover to cover without a break, beginning in the early evening and finishing at four in the morning. It was THAT good!

When we eventually read his book, *THUNDERBIRDS*, we were amazed that he remembered everything we said to him, word for word, that evening he joined us for dinner. He hadn't taken any notes at all. As a matter of fact, he never took any notes during the entire six weeks that he was with the team! A gifted mind like his only comes down the pike once in a million years… if that often.

Sometimes I'm asked to tell stories about my personal experiences while I was a Thunderbird. One story that stands out in my memory was our fifty-five day whirlwind tour of the Far East.

During November and December of 1959, we flew thirty-two performances throughout Okinawa, the Philippines, Taiwan, Japan and Hawaii for a total combined audience of 4,624,000 people.

During our stay in the Philippines an incident in my past came back to haunt me.

It was during Philippine National Aviation Week that teams from Australia, Nationalist China, New Zealand, the United Kingdom and the Philippines performed demonstrations for a crowd of one million spectators. After the four hour show, all the pilots from all the teams gathered to meet each other and enjoy the post-show festivities.

During the meeting with the Australian team, I got the shock of my life!

Our team leader at that time was Major Fitz Fitzgerald who was introducing us to the Aussie team. None of the Aussies would shake my offered hand and their smiles vanished when they were introduced to me. Finally, the Aussie team leader looked me straight in the eye and said, "You're the dirty bugger that wiped a booger on our Chief of Staff."

After a few moments, to let his remark sink in, and noticing the dumbfounded look on my face, the Aussie team broke out in rollicking laughter. The Aussie team leader took great delight in telling my teammates, who knew nothing of my infamous deed, all about the incident… And added that the story is known to everyone in the Royal Australian Air Force!

During my two year tour with the Thunderbirds, Jeanne had to become a jack of all trades while taking care of two growing boys who seldom saw their Dad. My second year with the team, I was away from home three hundred and two days. We were never home for more than three days at a time.

On one occasion, when I was home, Jeanne and I overheard Shawn and his little buddy chatting. Shawn's buddy asked him, "What does your Daddy do?" Shawn replied, "Oh, he flies around the country blowing smoke out his tail." Neither Shawn, nor Chuckie, seemed impressed that their Dad was a member of the *Thunderbirds*.

The Thunderbird families always gathered along the flight line to greet us after a long absence. The wives had resigned themselves to the long absences which prompted one of them to remark as we taxied in, "Here come the horny bastards with their dirty laundry!"...She was right on both counts.

After two years on the team you could wind up with forty, or more, t-shirts, shorts and pairs of socks, because we were never in one place long enough to have laundry done. We simply bought new underwear along the way.

I've been asked many times what it's like to visit so many different and interesting places that the average person will never see in their lifetime. Although we performed in all fifty states, twice in many of them, plus Canada, Guatemala, Bermuda, Puerto Rico and the Far East, we seldom got to do what the average tourist did… which is see the sights.

Our time was taken up by doing TV appearances, visiting children's hospitals, doing press interviews, and at least one practice show every day. Our evenings were usually spent being wined and dined by hosts who went all out to insure that we enjoyed ourselves. As much as we appreciated their efforts, there were times when we all would have preferred a quiet dinner and some sack time.

Near the end of my two year tour we were in Puerto Rico, operating out of Ramey AFB, doing shows throughout the island. It was one of the few times that we had a little time off for ourselves. Neil Eddins, Bobby Janca, Herm Griffin and I were lounging around the Officers pool when we all looked up to see a strange aircraft that no one recognized. I thought it resembled an aircraft I saw back at Nellis years ago while leading a flight of students at the ACM (Air Combat Maneuvering) area at 40,000 feet.

Back in those days UFOs were on everybody's mind and we had orders to report anything that was not of this world. One of my students called out a 'bogey' three o'clock high. I didn't believe him until I caught a glimpse of what looked like a glider, ten to fifteen thousand feet above us, heading westerly toward our air to air gunnery ranges.

All thoughts of meeting another flight for a rip roaring mock air combat were forgotten. It appeared as though the strange bird was descending so I decided to follow it. It was still high above us when we reached the air-to-air ranges and had to break off and return to Nellis.

To the west of the air-to-air ranges was a place called Groom Lake. All sorts of weird things occurred there and no one was allowed to fly anywhere near the area. After landing at Nellis, I went directly to Base Ops and reported my sighting. The Ops officer filed my report, with the others, and I thought that was the end of it.

But at home that evening there was a knock on the door. When I opened the door there was a man in civilian clothes standing there who produced identification proving him to be an agent with the CIA. He told me that I did not see anything that day. I began describing what I saw and he interrupted me saying sternly, "Captain Maultsby, you didn't see a thing today!" I asked him in but he declined and turned to leave after saying, "You understand, you didn't see a thing!"... Well, it made sense. The strange bird was operating out of Groom Lake.

When the strange bird approached to land that day in Puerto Rico, Neil, Bobby, Herm and I decided to hop in a staff car and head for base ops to have a look. When we arrived at the parking ramp, the strange bird was nowhere in sight. Surely it couldn't have taken off without us hearing it.

We decided to climb up into the control tower, situated on top of a hangar, to ask the controllers what happened to the aircraft that had just landed. When we entered the hangar our question was answered. The strange bird was there, surrounded by a rope fence and being guarded by a fierce looking AP (Air Policeman) daring us to come any closer. We all quickly agreed we'd seen enough and headed back to the pool. I told the others the strange bird looked like the aircraft I reported as a UFO a while back.

That evening, while having dinner in the Officers mess, we were approached by a dapper looking gentleman dressed in civilian attire who asked if he could join us. He introduced himself as Bobby Gardiner and said he recognized the Thunderbird insignia we all wore on our blazers. He didn't offer to state his business, or affiliations, which aroused our curiosity. We asked him if he had anything to do with the aircraft that landed this afternoon and was now being guarded in the Base Ops hangar. He admitted to being the pilot, but would say no more about the aircraft, or his mission. After I mentioned that I had seen a similar aircraft a few years ago northwest of Nellis AFB, he did not respond, and then remembered he was late for a previous engagement.

Before leaving he asked, "By the way, who will be completing their tour with the Thunderbirds next?" I told him that I would be completing my tour in a few months. He bid us goodnight and left.

It wasn't until after Francis Gary Powers was shot down over Russia on May 6th, 1960 that the mystery was solved. For weeks thereafter the newspapers and magazines carried stories about the secretive U-2 spy plane. That guy that we met in Puerto Rico, Bobby Gardiner, was flying a U-2!

During the summer of 1960 the T-birds were scheduled for a show at Laughlin AFB in Del Rio, Texas. We all now knew it was the home of the 4080th Strategic Reconnaissance Wing and the U-2 aircraft. We looked forward to doing the show there and perhaps get a closer look at a U-2.

But there wasn't a U-2 in sight when we landed at Laughlin, just a few T-33s and U-3As. We were greeted by almost everybody on base, from the Wing Commander on down. As I was climbing out of my cockpit I saw a Captain headed for my aircraft who turned out to be Bobby Gardiner. Following introductions, and after settling into the VOQ (Visiting Officers Quarters), Captain Gardiner informed me that his squadron Commander wanted to talk to me in his office.

Lt. Col. Buzz Curry wasted no time getting to the point. He asked me if I would like to join his outfit when my tour with the T-birds ended. Every pilot in the squadron was a volunteer and no one could be assigned against his will. I tried asking questions about their mission, but Lt. Col. Curry evaded them. I stated that I would have to get Jeanne's opinion before making a commitment. He assured me there was no hurry about a decision, and to let him know a month before I left the T-birds.

I'd learned before this meeting with Curry that Gary Powers worked for the agency (CIA), and was making $30,000 a year. I wasn't interested in flying a powered glider, but I would gladly fly a barn door for that kind of money!

Bobby Gardiner led me to believe that the 4080th Squadron was flying the same missions as the agency and the pay was good. I asked him if the 4080th was a SAC outfit, he hedged by saying the squadron was assigned to SAC for support only. The last thing I wanted to do was join a SAC outfit when I could pick any fighter unit in the U.S. Air Force.

We left Laughlin without seeing a U-2, which were in hangars where no one was allowed to enter. All the hush-hush and half answered questions made me think I should forget about joining an outfit that couldn't level with you for security reasons. My top secret clearance had been no advantage at all. All of the pilots I met at Laughlin were equally evasive. But they did seem proud to be in such an elite outfit.

Weeks went by and I'd given up the idea of joining the U-2 outfit when Bobby Gardiner landed at Nellis in a T-33 with a SAC emblem painted on its fuselage. I hadn't discussed Lt. Col. Curry's offer with Jeanne, because I didn't intend to accept it. I will always regret having invited Bobby to stay the weekend with us. After swearing us to secrecy, he convinced both of us that joining the U-2 outfit would dramatically improve our lives. Money was the only incentive for me, but he hinted at things unheard of in the regular Air Force. We were doing nicely on a Captain's pay, but more money is always nicer.

After Bobby left, Jeanne and I agonized over the prospect of passing on an assignment to Germany for an unknown future. There were still too many unknowns regarding Bobby's glowing account of being a U-2 pilot that troubled me. But we finally decided to give it a try.

I asked Major Fitzgerald if I could leave in August in order to get Chuckie enrolled in school in Del Rio. Besides that, Captain Bob Cass couldn't wait to take my place.
The word spread around Nellis that I was taking an assignment with a U-2 outfit stationed in Del Rio, Texas. Two guys in particular, Major Jack Brown, who was my gunnery teammate at the William Tell meet, and Captain Hank Buttleman, an Ace in Korea, were interested and wanted to know why I took the assignment.

They couldn't understand why a fighter jock would want to fly a powered glider. I was about as evasive as Lt. Col. Curry and Bobby had been in answering questions, not because I wanted to be, but because I flat out didn't know myself. This aroused their curiosity even more I'm sure. I told them that as soon as I got to Laughlin and got clued in that I would clue them in.

*   *   *

Chapter 8

The Cost of Glory

Captain Charles "Fish" Salmon was, as one of the Thunderbirds' wives put it, "A terrific looking guy who made women stop and turn around." We pilots only thought of Fish behind the stick, but that was thinking enough. For Fish Salmon was one of those men who are called great pilots. He started with the Thunderbirds in January of 1958, worked as a Solo Pilot through most of October, and when Sam Johnson completed his tour, began to fly the Slot.

People instinctively liked the guy. He looked like a Hollywood version of a fighter pilot; handsome, winning smile, that sort of thing. He was six foot one and weighed about 210 pounds; a big, happy guy who had a tremendous sense of humor. As a solo pilot, he was almost the twin brother of Griff.

He had flair, timing, and the execution of his maneuvers were cut with a razor they were so precise.

I learned that Fish didn't take kindly to being stifled, and he had his own way of pressing home a point. During a show at Eglin Air Force Base, "home territory" without flying restrictions, Fish wanted to open the show with a supersonic pass. He had been held back on this so long he was aching to come before a crowd on the deck with the bird wide open and howling.

To our astonishment the local brass poured cold water on the idea. "There are too many sonic booms going on here all the time," one officer snapped. "It's about time we started to put a halt to this nonsense."

Now this is a strange statement. Eglin is a proving ground, and there is a constant war under way here. Observers to the Aerial Firepower Demonstrations at Eglin have seen more shooting going on than a good many veterans of actual combat. The din at times becomes deafening, with supersonic strikes, cannon, machine guns, napalm, high explosives, and simulated atomic blasts being the order of the day.

Fish didn't say a word, but he set his jaw in a way that foretold that he just might alter his opening pass slightly. As he explained to the team before the show, "It was a good time to teach a few people a lesson or two."

At Eglin, the proving ground personnel mark a large, clear white line with chalk dust along the ground. This moves from the rear right of the long reviewing stands, so that an airplane approaches from this position, passes directly in front of the crowd, but goes away to its front left. With so many planes coming in with all their armament blasting away, the chalk line is a vital reference point that erases all positioning doubts for the pilot. The brass pointed out the line to Fish, told him to scrub the supersonic pass, and to fly over that line with the "afterburner opening."

Fish took his fighter to barely three feet off the deck. Just under supersonic speed, he rocketed without warning (except to air traffic control) from the left rear of the crowd, afterburner blasting on and off in a series of crashing explosions. Fish was so low as he beat up the deck that every time he slammed the throttle into AB a streamer of fire lashed the ground, sending chalk flying in all directions in clouds of white dust.

The thousands of people in the reviewing stands watched breathlessly as Fish shot across their view. Usually the solo man makes his pass to the end of the field or a designated line, then hauls up and around in a swooping, steep, climbing left turn. But Fish reached his line for the pull-up, and just kept right on going. He dragged the Super Sabre away from the reviewing stands, still at his three foot height, and disappeared into the fields beyond, the afterburner still blasting-BOOM, then silence; then, another BOOM, and silence, and again, and again.

The crowed jumped to its feet. Six thousand people stared in amazement (except Dick Crane, who was almost fit to be tied at the reaction of the audience), and every one of them, including pilots in attendance, was convinced that Fish was going to prang that bird right into a wall of trees. But at the last possible second (it seemed that way; Fish had plenty of room), the fighter lifted her nose and screamed skyward in a tremendous, soaring left chandelle. It looked death-defying and all that, but it wasn't; rather it was a combination of superb flying, precise timing, and all the effects of optical illusion because of the increasing distance.

The timing was the most important thing, because as 6,000 people kept their eyes glued to the hurtling solo airplane, Robby led us, the diamond, over their heads directly from the back of the crowd. And just as we crossed over all four of us lit the afterburners.

Narrator Dick Crane said it was the most marvelous sight of a crowd He'd ever seen. The four afterburners went off like a salvo of giant bombs directly over the reviewing stand and that audience (half of them military pilots) just collapsed back into their seats. We called that episode the day of the famous One-Two.

On March 12th, 1959, the team was practicing in our own private amphitheater of Thunderbird Lake. We had flown the entire demonstration and then came down on the deck, using an old dirt road as a reference line, to practice precision pitchouts for landing. Fitz was the new leader and had recently taken the reins from Robby.

It was a good practice session, and we came in for the pitchout in a solid diamond formation. Halfway down the 'runway,' at a height of one hundred feet, Fitz pitched up and out cleanly to the left, swinging into the steep vertical bank that brings him into his tight 180-degree turn.

Exactly one second behind the leader, Gayle Williams (then flying Left Wing) snapped his wings over and followed. Next I came hard on Gayle's tail and finally flying in trail, coming out of the slot, was Fish Salmon.

It's difficult to fit everything into its exact place because of the speed, timing and G-forces involved, but it seemed almost certain that Fish came out of the diamond a little too fast and just a bit hard. I was watching the airplanes in front of me and couldn't see Fish as he rolled into his pitch-out; Fish, in turn, positioned himself on me.

Both of us were in our vertical banks, pulling those punishing Gs, when suddenly Fish saw that he was over-running me and in another second would collide with me with his airplane. The instant that Fish noticed his excessive closing speed, he reacted. He tried desperately to dump full stick and to kick hard rudder. This was a top rudder movement, tramping down on the right rudder in the left bank, which would move him off and away from my fighter.

But despite his instant reactions, the minute error of judgment was compounded by speed and the one-second pitchout interval into an inevitable collision. Actually, Fish moved so quickly the other pilots later said it was an almost impossible pilot reaction, it was so fast. And the attempted corrective action saved Fish from entangling both of our airplanes in mass of wreckage that would have killed both of us.

The margin of a complete miss, or a collision, narrowed down to just about a tenth of a second. But Fish didn't have that fraction of time and he couldn't skid his airplane clear. Despite his frantic efforts, momentum carried him almost in front of my fighter.

The F-100 just missed slamming broadside into my fighter; instead, it struck a glancing blow. Fish's vertical stabilizer hit my Super Saber at the long pitot boom and the nose scoop. The impact ripped away the pitot boom, leaving me with no airspeed reading, and also damaging the underside of the nose scoop.

I felt a sudden vibration; pieces of metal and parts of the boom ripped back through the intake into the engine. Almost in the same instant, the force of the impact hurled my fighter out of control into a half-cartwheel.

As the big airplane whirled on its wing, I heard clearly in my earphones the distressed voice of Fish: "I've hit Chuck!" He seemed absolutely disgusted with himself for committing an error that he felt was unforgivable; and relief was obvious a moment later when I snapped my airplane back into level flight.

The collision sheared the top eighteen inches of the vertical stabilizer from Fish's airplane. We both had our planes back in level flight immediately. And Fish wisely pulled back on the stick and went into a fast climb.

The other pilots reacted like a well-oiled machine moving through a dress rehearsal. Gayle Williams skidded in to take up the wingman's position so that he could visually check the damage. Homer Whitlow, flying that day as an observer for my final checkout for the Right Wing position, immediately lit his afterburner and rocketed after Salmon's climbing airplane. Hot on his tail was Fitz, who had racked his airplane around in a wicked turn to reach his Slot man.

Williams radioed that he had me under control, that the airplane was flyable, and in no immediate danger. The F-100C was under full control, and Williams stayed glued to my wings, calling out the air speeds. We headed back to Nellis, flying a wide pattern in formation, and landing as though we were tied together.

Fish, of course, wanted altitude. At 30,000 feet he leveled off and set his course for Nellis. The closer he got to home, the better. He didn't know the full extent of the damage to his airplane, and although it responded well enough to the controls, it vibrated badly through the rear section. Altitude was insurance to get back to Nellis, and if necessary, to eject from a safe height.

Fitz checked out Salmon's airplane from every possible angle. Despite the vibration, she continued to fly, and Fish reported normal control response was being maintained. All engine instruments operated normally, he had no power loss. Except for that vibration, he seemed to be in good shape.

"Thunderbird Leader from Four," Fish called, "I think I can bring this bear in. She seems alright. I'll lower the gear and drop her back to approach speed to check the reaction...." By following this procedure at 30,000 feet, Fish assured himself plenty of room to recover from any unusual response of the airplane to his lowered airspeed. Whitlow and Fitz dropped back and to each side to fly a loose trail, watching every move that Fish made. Nellis was in sight; about twenty miles to the southeast of the airplanes, right over the last ridges, when Fish eased back the power and lowered the gear. He was going to fly the full approach procedure at altitude with the throttle back and the gear down; if the fighter responded well, there would be no problem in saving the airplane. Fish called out every move he made in the cockpit.

The other pilots reduced power with him, decelerating to the same speed. At 225 knots Fish lowered the gear. Just as the right wheel was halfway out of the well, and the left gear was a third out of the well and coming down, the airplane reacted to the sudden change in pressure and airflow. Coupled with the loss of the upper vertical stabilizer, the fighter got away from Salmon; the loss of the top of the vertical stabilizer proved too much to maintain control.

Instantly the F-100C pitched up to the right, whipped over on her back, and then whirled into a spin….
At once Fish snapped up the gear and started his spin recovery. Fitz and Whitlow were in a wide spiral about the spinning airplane, hauling it in close to watch everything that was happening. By the time he had dropped to 23,000 feet, Fish appeared to be in control again, and seemed to be just about out of the spin.

But suddenly the nose pitched up violently again, and she clawed over and into another spin. Fish fought her out of it the second time, but again she broke away and entered a third spin. In seconds the fighter fell below 20,000 feet. Whitlow called anxiously, "How is she flying, Fish? Can you get her out of the spin? Can you recover? Keep your eyes on your altitude! If you can't bring her out of that spin, give yourself plenty of time to bail out."

Fish called Fitz. "I'd like to stay with this bear for a couple of more recoveries, Boss. I can get her out of this spin…."

Twice more Fish brought her out, and twice more there came the violent pitch up and the whip into the spin. When the three airplanes passed through 15,000 feet, Fitz decided that this was more than enough.

"Get ready to get out of that thing, Fish." Homer repeated the message, more and more concerned with the vanishing height. The big Super Saber whirled sickeningly through four more turns.

"Fish, let it go!" Fitz ordered. "Get out of there, bail out, NOW!"

Fish didn't waste any time. Immediately after Fitz's call, the canopy blew off the airplane. It was followed at once by Fish in the seat. In the next moment he disappeared from Fitzgerald's sight, behind his airplane. But Homer Whitlow was right there as Fish fell out of sight from Fitz.

What no one knew was that Fish didn't have a chance to switch his parachute mechanism from the zero lanyard position for low altitude flight to the one-second setting for greater heights. Immediately after the collision he had climbed to altitude; in his preoccupation with checking out the airplane the detail escaped him. In the spin, it was impossible to change the setting, for centrifugal force from his rapid rotation prevented the movement.

Homer saw the parachute stream out. But it did not open fully. He watched Fish in the partially-opened chute fall out of sight. Homer never saw Fish separate from his seat; he kept watching, but nothing happened.

We're not sure of what happened, not exactly. But because

of the chute opening instantly, and the effects of the spin… well, whatever it was, for some unknown reason the heavy seat drifted up and tore right through the canopy. The chute never opened fully, although it did slow Fish's decent.

Fish Salmon, unfortunately, had run out of luck. Actually, everyone at this time was convinced that Fish had made a successful ejection. Even as he was blown free of the spinning fighter, Fitz ordered a helicopter dispatched on emergency call from Nellis. His parachute streaming behind him, Fish fell for three miles.

At the base we heard only that Fish had bailed out and that a chopper was on its way to pick him up and bring him back. We didn't know at the time that Captain Ted Baer, the flight surgeon assigned to the team, was the doctor on crash duty that day, and was in the chopper flying to the scene.

Fitz and Homer were circling the area where the plane crashed, and they were trying to locate Fish by his white parachute. While they looked for their pilot, Baer was coming in. The doc didn't know the details, didn't know who was down. Only that the bird was from Nellis.
Fitz and Homer were running low on fuel. The moment they saw the chopper moving in, they had to run for Nellis to land.

The helicopter crew searched the area around the crash scene. Then, several miles away, across the desert floor, the pilot saw a parachute. It was at the base of a 3,000 foot cliff. The fighter pilot, they saw, had landed at the bottom of a small range of hills. The helicopter dropped to the ground at the bottom of the hill, and Ted Baer and the crew started to rush up the steep incline. Baer is not a big man, but he scrambled up that rocky, sharp slope in fifteen minutes. It later took the experienced search-and-rescue parties thirty-five minutes to cover the same ground. Baer ran as fast as he could toward the body that he saw crumpled on the ground. He still didn't know who the man was.

But as he clambered breathlessly over the last boulder, he saw the Thunderbird helmet... Ted stopped as though he had been struck by a physical blow. The shock was terrific; it was then that he knew the crumpled form on the ground was one of *his* men.

A doctor in a business where a crash can, and usually does, mean a flaming horror becomes hardened to his job. At least they're supposed to be hardened. But Ted Baer admitted later that it took almost all his will power to force himself forward, then, to bend down, and turn the body over to see who it was.

He knew, from the moment he saw the body, that it couldn't be me, Fitzgerald, or Crane. It was a big man. The realization that it had to be Fish Salmon, Gayle Williams, or Homer Whitlow, flashed through his mind.

Then he discovered, with mounting shock and horror, that the body in his arms was that of one of his closest friends. Without thinking, he immediately checked for pulse and heartbeat. He stood up slowly. Fish was beyond all earthly help.

Ted stumbled to the nearest rock and sat down, his senses

were numb. He fought to keep the tears from coming out of his eyes. He was still there, numbed by grief, when the rest of the party found them. It took the rescue crew an hour to return the body to the helicopter.

They flew back to Nellis Air Force Base with the only pilot who had ever been lost to the Thunderbirds.

*   *   *

Chapter 9

U-2 and Me

I knew I was going to miss the fighter business, especially Nellis, but it was time to be moving on. Jeanne was looking forward to a change even though it wouldn't be Germany. Chuckie and Shawn would miss their friends at Nellis, but they would make new friends soon enough at Laughlin.

The T-birds went all out to make our departure a memorable one. We'll never forget our going away party at our favorite steakhouse about twenty miles north of Vegas on the Tonopah highway. We left Nellis the morning of Sept.11th, 1960 in our 1958 Chevy station wagon headed for Del Rio, Texas. We stopped overnight in Las Cruces, New Mexico, got off to a late start the next day, arriving in Del Rio around 2100 hours. Jeanne wanted to drive through town before we went out to the base; this took exactly one minute.

On Main Street there was a Sears catalog store, a jewelry store, movie theater, furniture store and a dry goods store. There wasn't much else on those two downtown blocks. I overheard Jeanne mutter, "Looks like my shopping days are over." I tried to cheer her up by pointing out that San Antonio was only a two hour drive from here.

Bobby Gardiner had arranged a guest house for us to stay in until our furniture arrived and we were assigned permanent quarters. We checked into the guest house where Bobby had left a note stating that he'd give a call at 0800 then meet us at the Officers Club for breakfast with a few other pilots.

Bobby and his wife, Laura, along with several other couples, gave us a warm welcome and made us feel at home. Incidentally, Laura had been a WASP (Womens Auxiliary Service Pilot) during World War II and had flown every fighter and bomber in the inventory.

After breakfast we were given a tour of Laughlin. We were impressed with the base housing and the many recreational facilities. Jackie Loden, the wife of one of the navigators in the squadron, was especially helpful in getting us squared away. She helped Jeanne enroll Chuckie in the Catholic school in town, but Shawn wasn't school age yet.

There were only a few pilots and navigators lounging around when we visited squadron ops. Even Lt./Col. Curry was absent. Bobby explained that most of the pilots and navigators were TDY (temporary duty) at an OL (operating location) somewhere overseas. Of course, he wouldn't say where.

After the squadron tour, I thought it was about time to get some straight answers about the assignment that had been evaded so far. What Bobby admitted literally made me sick. Yes, this was a SAC Wing, no, we are not with the agency, but sometimes pilots were recruited by the agency, and no, there isn't a $30,000 a year salary. Well, my greed had certainly gotten me into a hellova fix! Why had he purposely misled me, what could be the reason? I found out later.

I dreaded having to tell Jeanne the truth about the assignment. After all, she could be enjoying herself in Germany. However, she took the bad news like the trooper she was saying, "Well, we're here, so let's make the best of it."

Making the best of it took quite a bit of doing for me. I went from flying a supersonic jet twice a day, with a world renowned aerobatics demonstration team based in Las Vegas, directly to flying a T-33 twice a month at a secret base in a remote area of West Texas. I didn't even fly the remainder of September.

The last of the very sparse flights in a T-33 was on November 18th and was originally planned as a cross-country to log instruments and night time. My new friend and neighbor, Captain Joe Hyde, and I would be flying to Nellis and RON (remain-over-night) to meet up with Hank Buttleman and Jack Brown to let them know that the U-2 outfit was not what I was led to believe it was. Then the plan changed.

As I was leaving to meet Joe at the squadron to plan our flight, the phone rang. It was a call from the next door neighbor of my Aunt and Uncle's in Norfolk. She told me my Aunt had died in her sleep. She hadn't complained of any illness the night before. It was a shock to Uncle Louis who was taking it very hard and asked the neighbor, Mrs. Krise, to call to ask if I could come to Norfolk. I assured her I would be there in a few hours. Joe did the flight planning while I arranged for emergency leave. Joe would drop me off in Norfolk and fly back to Laughlin.

After my Aunt's funeral I helped Uncle Louie get his affairs in order. I could see he wouldn't last long without my Aunt who had done everything for him, enabling his dependency on alcohol. He'd been an alcoholic for many years. I suggested that he close up the house, leave the key with Mrs. Krise, and come to Texas to stay with us for a while. He readily consented. I called Jeanne to ask what she thought of the idea. She thought his being around family and away from that home full of memories would be good for him.

Prior to leaving Norfolk in Uncle Louie's 1953 Mercury, a flock of vultures descended upon the house. I was appalled at the behavior some their best friends exhibited. One friend wanted Uncle Louis to trade refrigerators since he wouldn't be needing the big new one he had because he was now single. Another life-long friend of my Aunt's went all through the house like a woman possessed, grabbing anything she pleased! She claimed my Aunt had promised that she could have this and that if anything ever happened to her. I stood about all I could take from those two, and others, and finally heaved the lot of them out the door.

All the while Uncle Louis was high as a Georgia pine and couldn't have cared less if they stripped the house bare… if I hadn't been there.

During the trip back to Texas I was having misgivings about bringing Uncle Louie to stay with us. Although I never saw him nipping from the bottle it was obvious that he indeed nipped, judging by the stench of alcohol in the car. While in heavy traffic going through a town in Louisiana, I had to break hard suddenly to avoid rear-ending the car in front of me. Out from under his seat rolled a fifth of *Old Overholt* whiskey. He pretended to be as surprised as I was and asked, "How in the hell did that get there?" I answered, "Impy must have put it there." Impy was his big Boxer dog that was stretched out sleeping on the back seat.

I did all of the driving during our three day trip while Uncle Louie sang, "When Irish Eyes Are Smiling," until I knew it by heart. You always knew he was very drunk if he broke out in a song. It helped some that he actually had a good tenor voice.

Our house on base was a duplex with a large living room, a large kitchen with a walk-in pantry, three bed rooms and two baths. Chuckie and Shawn shared a bedroom so Uncle Louie could have his own room.

 For a while we were hoping we could help him kick his drinking habit with perhaps the help of A.A. He, of course, considered himself only a heavy social drinker… only alcoholics went to A.A.

Back at Laughlin I spent my time between infrequent T-33

or U-3A flights by attending ground school covering courses in celestial navigation, miscellaneous U-2 systems and numerous intelligence gathering devices. At 65,000 feet, objects two inches in diameter were discernible and interpretable on the ground. There were other intelligence gathering devices that could be installed in the Q-bay instead of the cameras. The Q-bay was located just aft of the cockpit and forward of the main landing gear. If no devices were installed in the Q-bay, like when the aircraft was to be flown on a training or ferry flight, then comparable weight had to be installed. We called the weight device a 'glockenspiel.'

The ground school was usually conducted by a U-2 pilot/instructor and a navigator. Often times a tech-rep (technical representative) from the companies that manufactured the various devices would give demonstrations using mock-ups. During the remainder of 1961 there were only three of us attending the slow paced ground school, Captain Dave Ray, Captain Pinky Primrose and me.

If you're wondering why the T-33 and U-3A were used in the U-2 program… The T-33 was used for instrument checks and cross country flights. Every pilot had to accumulate a prescribed amount of take offs and landings, instrument time, actual weather time, night time and be jet qualified. The U-3A was used as a chase plane when a pilot first checked out in a U-2, and to simulate the U-2s approach pattern and landing speed. A T-33 couldn't be used in those roles. Later in the 1960s, a two place U-2 was manufactured to make it possible for an IP to ride along in the rear cockpit to monitor a student pilot.

After completing ground school, and after passing the oral and written exams, the next step to becoming a U-2 pilot was to be suited out in a MC-3 high altitude partial pressure suit and MA-2 helmet. This took place at Carswell AFB near Ft. Worth, Texas where they had a high altitude pressure chamber.

The pressure chamber personnel told me that many aspiring U-2 pilots threw in the towel after two days of the suit and chamber. If I could have gone back to the fighter business I might have done the same thing. But once in SAC... how does the saying go?... "From the womb to the tomb."

The suiting out process took several days so I took Jeanne and Shawn along to see Ft. Worth. We left Chuckie with Uncle Louie, or vice versa. Jackie Loden, who lived across the street, assured us she would keep an eye on things and see to it that Chuckie made it to school and back.

The drive to Ft Worth via San Antonio, Austin and Waco was amazing to Jeanne, who thought all of Texas was tumbleweeds, sand and sage brush. Most of Texas, especially the hill country, is beautiful. After checking into the VOQ at Carswell AFB we visited the Psychological Training Unit where I would be fitted for a high altitude pressure suit and undergo several chamber rides. Since I was the only customer for the several days the friendly chamber personnel invited Jeanne and Shawn to come along with me to observe all the procedures. They made our stay at Carswell memorably pleasant.

Being fitted for a partial pressure suit is an all-day process. They were tailor made since no two bodies are shaped the same. Imagine putting on a girdle that covered your neck down to your ankles… by yourself. White long johns were donned first, making sure there were no creases and that the seams were on the outside. The slightest crease could feel like a broomstick after seven or eight hours encased in the MC-3.

The MA-2 helmet was as equally uncomfortable as the suit. It had a rubber neck seal you pulled over your head so that it fit snug around your neck. Next came gloves and regular combat boots, plus a flight suit over the pressure suit. The whole fitting process was repeated for the second suit that became the spare. Both suits were pressure checked before I entered the pressure chamber. Inflatable tubes running along the sides of the arms, chest, thighs, and legs pulled the suits fabric tightly against your body to apply the pressure that would prevent certain death at high altitudes if your body wasn't protected. It was a sobering thought.

Other than being uncomfortably trussed up like a mummy, the chamber flights were completed without a hitch. I fully understood why some pilots quit the U-2 program at that point. So, having completed the suiting out process ahead of schedule, we stayed another day in Ft. Worth to see the sights.

Some of the pilots and navigators, who were TDY when we arrived, began returning to Laughlin. Other people we'd met since arriving would take their place and be gone for three months. I still wasn't privy to all that went on and wouldn't be until I successfully completed the U-2 checkout. They didn't want anyone who couldn't complete the training having knowledge of their classified missions.

After many hours in the Cessna U-3A (affectionately known as the "blue canoe," or "bug smasher") simulating the U-2 landing pattern, approach, and landing speeds; the day (January 10th, 1961) finally came for my check-out in the article known as the U-2.

I already had several hours of cockpit time and was acquainted with the instrumentation. I marveled at the simplicity of the aircraft. There were no frills or fads incorporated into its design. Any additional weight could adversely affect its maximum altitude.

The first flight was relegated to shooting six touch and go landings while being chased by a U-3A with an IP aboard. Another IP in the souped-up station wagon would sit at the threshold of the runway, then follow you down the runway calling your height above the runway. Five, four, three, two feet, hold it off, one foot, until you touched down on the main and tail gear in a full stall. If you stalled out too high and contacted the runway, you were sure to receive extensive damage. The U-2 was a very fragile aircraft. If you landed main gear first, a porpoise was sure to follow ("porpoise" being the word used to describe a landing where the main gear touches, skips, and bounces the aircraft back into the air).

The U-2 wasn't designed to perform well at low altitudes, but I was impressed with the flight characteristics. Besides the U-3A, the U-2 was the first aircraft I had flown that had a yoke on the control column. This didn't present a problem because I wasn't about to do a snap roll; in fact, a 30 degree bank was considered aerobatics in a U-2. After four more flights below 30,000 feet, came the day that I would see what a U-2 was all about.

My first flight in a U-2 wearing a partial pressure suit occurred on February 14th, 1961. The day before was spent flight planning for a six hour round robin flight. "Round robin" was the term used to describe a flight that originated from an airfield, flew a designated flight path and returned.

It usually took from five to six hours preparing maps while a navigator computed the celestial navigation fixes. Since the U-2 cockpit is cramped, to say the least, the maps or aeronautical charts were trimmed down so that four inches on either side of the intended flight path were all that was left. These were mounted on 8 X 12 inch cardboard sheets and it took eight to twelve sheets to accommodate the strip map.

Three hours prior to takeoff time you reported to the physiological support unit where you would have a meal consisting of steak and eggs, toast, juice and coffee. This high protein meal was intended to prevent activating your bowels. This has bowel activation has occurred to some hapless U-2 drivers who turned their pressure suits into poopy suits.

Following the meal a flight surgeon would take your blood pressure, temperature and weight. Next came the suiting up of all the flight gear with the assistance of the Life Support Technicians. After suiting up you took a seat in a recliner that was outfitted with oxygen and air pressure hoses. Your suit was inflated to checked for leaks and you went on pure oxygen for thirty minutes to an hour to denitrogenate your blood. This practice of 'pre-breathing' was later discontinued.

Thirty minutes prior to start engine time, you were

connected to a portable oxygen bottle and boarded a van for the ride to your aircraft. In the meantime another U-2 driver had pre-flighted your aircraft and was waiting to help strap you in the cockpit and call off the checklist. Start engine, taxi, and take off were accomplished to the second. No deviations were tolerated. Adhering to these exact times was necessary in order to be at the right place at the right time when a celestial fix was taken. Prior to take off roll, a tracker camera was actuated that would run constantly throughout the flight. The film would determine how closely you followed the intended flight path.

The takeoff was about the only part of the flight I enjoyed. The Pratt & Whitney J-57 engine (the same engine used in the F-100) provided plenty of thrust so climb angles of between 60 and 65 degrees were the norm. It usually took thirty to thirty-five minutes to reach 65,000 feet. From there, as the fuel is burned off, the U-2 will cruise climb to above 70,000 feet.

Although the sextant is the primary means of navigation, time and distance navigation is made possible because there is little, or no, winds at altitude. Hitting a check point right on the second was not unusual. The auto-pilot enabled the pilot to operate the sextant and a myriad of other tasks that the mission called for. Another essential device was the drift sight; a glass bubble located on the underside of the fuselage, just forward of the cockpit, containing a scanning prism that enabled the pilot to scan the terrain from horizon to horizon, 360 degrees.

Upcoming check points could be identified miles away. It would have been somewhat impossible to follow a flight line without it.

My first flight above 70,000 feet seemed to go by quickly. I was kept busy with the sextant taking one or two observations on each leg of the flight. I didn't notice the discomfort the pressure suit caused until I started a letdown to land. I figured I would eventually get used to the suit, but for now... "Get me out of this thing!" When my helmet was finally removed, at least a cup of sweat drained out of the neck seal, which helped to explain why I lost four pounds on that flight.

Subsequent missions above 70,000 feet eventually became routine and I did get used to the pressure suit. After several more flights above 70,000 feet, I was given a standardization and evaluation flight check and awarded a crew member. A crew member meant you were fully qualified to participate in all missions throughout the world. Once you received a crew member it was next to impossible to be assigned to another outfit for the duration of your tour. My chances of getting back into fighters became nil.

Shortly after receiving a crew member I again asked Bobby Gardiner why in hell I was asked to join the U-2 program. He finally admitted that there was a friendly competition between the squadron commander and the group commander to see who could recruit single engine pilots versus multi-engine pilots. The squadron commander fancied himself to be a fighter pilot (only God knows why) and the group commander was a dyed in the wool bomber jock. The squadron commander thought that it would be coup de gras to not only recruit a fighter pilot, but an ex-Thunderbird. Bobby had to confess that he was sorry to have been part of the ridiculous scheme. Had it not been for that chance meeting in Puerto Rico, I'd still be in fighters and probably in Germany.

Jeanne and the boys were thoroughly enjoying themselves at Laughlin, which made it easier to bear the fact that I had screwed-up royally. With both boys now in school she had time for herself. She leased a horse from the base riding stable and became a good rider. She spent hours grooming her new pet. She took flying lessons at the base aero club.

I was glad to see her get out of the house more and told her so, whereupon she told me she needed to get out of the house if only to be away from Uncle Louie when the boys and I were gone. She considered him to be a repulsive alcoholic and a lecherous old bullshitter whom she did not trust to behave himself.

That did it! I wasn't going to leave her in jeopardy another minute and told Uncle Louie to leave… Now! Our friends couldn't understand how I could treat a kindly old soul so shabbily. But they didn't know about the numerous times that the APs (Air Police; the kids called them Apes) would show up at the door, at all hours of the night, bringing Uncle Louie home from one binge or another. He often would pass himself off as a senior CIA agent in town and take advantage of new admirers one way or another. He hooked up with an Airman on base who was headed back East and agreed to drive him to Norfolk. We all would miss his dog, Impy.

Jeanne and I were invited to a Thunderbird reunion taking place in Las Vegas in June of 1961. We'd become good friends with our neighbors directly across the street from us, Captain Joe Hyde and is wife Marianne, and asked them to come along for a stay at the *Riviera Hotel*. They were all for it of course. We arranged to have the boys stay with the Loden family across the street for the four days we'd be gone.

We intended to rent a Cessna 172 from the base aero club but none were available. Joe knew of a North American Navion that was available, but he had to go pick it up at Randolph AFB. He hitched a ride to Randolph in a U-3A and brought back the sorriest aircraft I'd ever seen. I asked a mechanic to give it a once over just to be safe. The maintenance records were in order, so other than needing a wash and new paint, he declared it to be airworthy.

The flight from Laughlin to El Paso went smoothly, but between El Paso and Phoenix we lost our radio. I was in the left seat with Joe as co-pilot. Jeanne and Marianne were in the back seats chatting away without a care in the world.

A mile from the Phoenix Sky Harbor Airport I started rocking my wings and lowered my landing gear to advise the tower that our radio was inoperative and we wanted to land. We got a green light and just as we began the runway approach, the engine stopped dead… frozen. The prop didn't move an inch. I dumped the nose and immediately started a left descending turn hoping to make a 360 degree turn and land. All pilots practice flame out patterns as a matter of course, but I'd never done one in a Navion. After 180 degrees of turn I noticed crash vehicles racing toward the runway. Evidently the tower noticed the frozen prop and alerted them. Airspeed and altitude are a pilots best friends in an emergency and I had both, so I wasn't too concerned about making a safe landing. If I continued the present rate of descent, airspeed, and radius of turn, I

I figured I'd touch down about 2,000 feet down the runway.

I breathed a sigh of relief when the main gear touched, but neither Joe, nor I, said a word until we came to a complete stop. Joe slid the canopy back to talk to the emergency crew who were preparing to tow us off the runway. When I looked in back to see how the girls were doing, it was obvious that they were totally unaware of what just happened and remained deep in conversation... which was a good thing.

We remained in the Navion while it was being towed to the parking ramp. The temperature was well over 100 degrees, so by the time we parked we were all wringing wet from sweat. After helping the girls deplane, Joe and I checked the oil dip stick that showed no oil at all! We looked under the fuselage and saw that it was drenched in oil. The oil pressure gauge had given no hint at all of the trouble ahead. Joe contacted the aero club at Randolph AFB and told them where they could find their Navion.

We'd had enough excitement for one day and decided to check into a motel at the airport. After dinner we were in the lounge enjoying a few toddies when I asked, "Do you know what would have happened if we had lost that engine five or ten minutes earlier?" Of course Joe knew but left it up to the girls to respond. After thinking on it a few seconds they both responded in unison, "Oh my God!" Jeanne then held up her glass and said, "Chalk up another one to your guardian angel Charlie." I just hoped I wouldn't run out of chalk.

The next morning we booked a commercial flight to

Vegas scheduled to leave that afternoon. We remembered there were several bottles of liquor in the baggage compartment of the Navion. Joe and I went out to the plane on the parking ramp, climbed onto the wing, and slid back the canopy. The stench emanating from the cockpit was bad enough to gag a maggot! The bottles of rum, bourbon and scotch had exploded because of the searing Arizona heat. The battery had also overflowed mixing acid with booze. Between the frozen engine and the stench in the cockpit, it wasn't likely that the Randolph aero club would ever want the Avion back.

We proceeded to Las Vegas via Frontier Airlines and checked into the Riviera Hotel. The next two days were spent taking in a Thunderbird demonstration, attending a ball at the Officers Club, attending another ball at the Riviera sponsored by North American Aviation, eating, drinking and being merry. Joe and Marianne had the best time of their lives and hated to see the party end. They also expressed wonder at how we could have traded this lifestyle for the one in Del Rio.

Upon arriving back at Laughlin, I was scheduled to replace a pilot at our OL (operating location) in Alaska. There was a network of OLs covering the globe. During July, August and September I would be flying out of Eielson AFB, Alaska on missions sponsored by the Defense Atomic Support Agency. The project known as HASP (High Altitude Sampling Program) was conducted to determine the quantity of radioactive material being ejected into the atmosphere from nuclear explosions. I flew eleven missions during those three months in Alaska and I never really got used to the ever-present sunshine.

Jeanne wrote several times a week keeping me informed of all the happenings on base and in town. A letter arrived in early August announcing that I would be a proud papa again in March. We had planned to try for a girl in a couple more years, but the weekend in Vegas, and all the Seagram 7, moved the plan ahead.

I returned in late September by ferrying a U-2 back to Laughlin while my replacement flew up in another one. My Q-bay was packed full of ten pound bricks of Alaskan King Crab. It was absolutely expected that a returning U-2 driver from Alaska would have crab on board and a committee was always present to purchase the bricks.

I wasn't scheduled for another OL until October of 1962. In the mean time I flew several photographic missions out of Laughlin that I can't discuss here.

Jeanne's pregnancy progressed without complications thanks to her gynecologist, Doctor Shien, who was a stickler for keeping unnecessary weight off of his patients. He would threaten to hospitalize anyone who gained more weight that he deemed appropriate. Jeanne co-operated fully to avoid being hospitalized. She delivered a healthy baby boy... again, on March 15th, 1962. We named him Kevin Durane (Durane being the original French spelling of her maiden name).

I was waiting outside the delivery room when a nurse came out to show me the ugliest baby I had ever seen! His little forehead sloped back just above his eyebrows at a very steep angle similar to a Neanderthal. The nurse noticed my horrified stare and assured me he would look normal the next day.

Jeanne was alert and eager to hear what I thought of my newest son when they brought her into the waiting room. She had already seen him so there was no use in lying. I said, "Well, it's about time we got an ugly one." With that, she burst out laughing. I was thinking there was nothing funny about having an ugly baby when Dr. Shien entered the waiting room and held Kevin up for me to see again and remarked, "Yep, his old man can't deny him!"

A good friend of ours, Captain Maybelle France, who was a nurse on duty that day, dropped by to see the new arrival and explained that Kevin had been delivered 'sunny side up,' which explained the misshapen forehead. I was again reassured that my new son would look normal the next day… but I wasn't so sure.

Chuckie and Shawn were thrilled to have a new brother, but had to wait three days to see him because kids weren't allowed in maternity wards in those days. In the meantime Kevin's head did shape up and he became a handsome little fella after all. The day we brought Kevin home there was a fight between Chuckie and Shawn over who would be the one to carry Kevin into the house. The issue was settled by a flip of a coin. Chuckie carried Kevin into the house and placed him on the same platform rocker that he'd placed Shawn on seven years before.

The first thing Jeanne did when she got home was try on a favorite dress she wore before getting pregnant. It fit perfectly. She later thanked Dr. Shien for being so adamant about not gaining excess weight. Fortunately, I didn't have to go TDY for five months so I got to watch Kevin go from a constantly sleeping infant to a happy and very alert five month old.

I was notified in late September that my second tour in Alaska was about to happen. I did not look forward to being in Alaska during the bitter cold months when the sun never shined. I would rather have flown missions out of our OL located in Australia where it's summer during our winter.

But back to Alaska I went aboard a KC-135 headed for Eielson AFB ...again. Lt./Col. Forest 'Whip' Wilson was the OL commander, Captain Don Webster, Captain 'Wee' Willie Lawson and myself were the U-2 drivers. The three navigators who did all of our flight planning were Captain Billie Bye, Captain Bob Yates and 1st/ Lt. Fred Okimoto.

The missions being flown were the same as before except we were now flying to the North Pole. Captain Don Webster was the first U-2 pilot to fly the 3,000 mile round trip to the Pole and back using celestial navigation all the way. The only radio beacon used was located at Barter Island. From there to the Pole was nothing but ice, stars and polar bears.

Willie Lawson was the next U-2 driver to fly up to the North Pole; my turn would come later. I sat in on all of the flight planning and briefings to be better prepared for when my turn came.

Unlike other HASP flights, these were accompanied by a Duck Butt flight as far as Barter Island where they would orbit and await your return. Duck Butt was a search and rescue team flying a Douglas DC4. If you were forced to bail out between Barter Island and the North Pole they would make every effort to locate you, even though the chances of doing so were slim to none.

The team said they could make one orbit before having to head for the nearest landfall. There was no use in having the para-rescue jumpers suffer the same fate as a downed pilot.

I asked one of the jumpers what he'd do if he had to jump over the Pole. He said, "I wouldn't pull the rip cord." I was sorry I asked and I still don't really know why they tagged along. They couldn't land on that jagged ice cap, and even if they did find you, by the time a ground party could reach you, you'd either be frozen solid, or decomposing in the belly of a polar bear.

Well, 'Wee' Willie didn't have any problems and returned from his flight with some of the most radioactive material collected to date. The Russians must have been popping off some mighty potent caps!

Things were heating up in Cuba right before I was to make a flight to the Pole. We heard that some of the U-2 drivers in our squadron were over flying Cuba to ascertain whether or not the Russians were off loading missiles onto Cuban soil. If they were, things could get dicey in a hurry.

On October 25th, 1962, the day before my flight to the Pole, Billie Bye, Fred Okimoto, Bob Yates and I were planning my flight. The same Duck Butt team sat in on the briefing that followed, but I didn't ask them any questions having learned that I didn't like their answers.

Since my take off was scheduled for midnight the 26th, I tried to get plenty of sleep during the day, but that was next to impossible. People were stomping in and out of the BOQ in their heavy snow boots all day. The harder I tried to sleep, the harder it became. I finally gave up and went down to the ops building and sacked out on a cot. No one would bother me there until three hours before my takeoff time.

I woke up at 8:00pm and went to the Officers mess for a breakfast of steak and eggs. Bob, Billie and Fred were there wondering where I was. They hadn't gotten much sleep either.

Pre-flight preparations were completed. I took off on time and proceeded to Barter Island. Duck Butt gave me a call on a pre-briefed frequency and said that we should both arrive over Barter Island at the same time. They wished me luck and said they would keep a light on in the window for me.

Over the Barter Island radio beacon, I set course for the Pole and prepared to take the first fix. It was right on the button! Those navigators were masters of their trade and everything went according to plan until I was halfway between Barter Island and the Pole.

Then streaks of light started dancing across the sky making it difficult to take a fix on the star I was shooting. I'd heard of the phenomena called Aurora Borealis, or Northern Lights, but I'd never seen them. They couldn't have appeared at a worse time and the further North I got, the more intense they became.

I held my heading and hoped the star I saw was the right one. The last few fixes before reaching the Pole, if in fact I had reached it, were highly suspect. I had no reason to believe I was off course, in spite of the suspect fixes. So I decided to go ahead and do a 90-270 degree turn at the determined time that would put me over the Pole. I turned left for 90 degrees, then immediately reversed the turn for 270 degrees until I was heading back along the same track, only in the opposite direction. This new track should have headed me straight for Barter Island.

I was out of range with Duck Butt, not that there was anything that they could do, but it would have been nice to hear a friendly voice. I had never flown over a land mass where you couldn't see a single light from horizon to horizon.

The first two fixes I took after leaving the Pole were wishful hoping and I was beginning to realize that something was terribly wrong. I began calling in the clear, hoping that someone out there might hear me and steer me in the right direction. I still thought I was on the right track for Barter Island, but the ETA (estimated time of arrival) was still some time away. It wasn't until I was out from under the Aurora Borealis effect that I knew I was off course… but which way? From the Pole, every direction is south.

I didn't bother with trying to take any more fixes. I would just fly time and distance and hope for the best.

I was three to four hundred miles North of Barter Island, or thought I was, when the first radio contact with Duck Butt was made. I even heard someone in our command post back at Eielson calling over the single sideband radio, but they couldn't receive my call. Surely I was in range of the radio beacon at Barter Island, but I couldn't pick it up. Had it shut down, or what?

As the ETA for Barter Island wound down to thirty minutes, Duck Butt called and said that they would start firing flares every five minutes commencing immediately. They were orbiting over Barter Island and advised me that the radio beacon was in operation and they were receiving it loud and clear. I didn't see a flare and asked them to fire another one. By this time I should be over Barter Island and should have been able to see a flare. They fired another one, but I did not see it! It was all I could do to fight off a panic attack! I was either many miles east or west of Barter Island... but which?

The navigator aboard Duck Butt called and asked me if I could identify a star. I told him I had the belt of Orion constellation about 15 degrees left of the nose of the aircraft. Several minutes later the navigator called and told me to steer 10 degrees left.

Almost immediately I received another call from an unknown source, using my call sign, telling me to turn 30 degrees right. What the hell is going on? The Duck Butt navigator didn't hear the latest call, so I knew I was unknown miles west of where I should be. I received another call from the unknown source telling me to turn right 35 degrees. I challenged him, using a code that only a legit operator would know, but there was no response.

Duck Butt called and asked me if I could see a glow on the eastern horizon. I replied negative. The transmissions from Duck Butt were getting weaker by the minute. The last one I heard was, "Turn left 15 degrees."

The transmissions from the unknown source were loud and clear, but I ignored them. I selected the emergency channel and broadcast, "MAY DAY! MAY DAY! MAY DAY!" as loud as I could.

I only had about thirty minutes of fuel left with no prospect of landing back at Eielson… or anywhere else! The U-2 carries enough fuel for nine hours and forty minutes of flight. I had been airborne for nine hours and ten minutes when suddenly I picked up a radio station directly off the nose of the aircraft. It came in loud and clear… and it sounded to me like Russian music. I then knew where I was!

The heretofore suppressed panic began to grip me. I didn't know whether to shit or go blind! I was sure of one thing though, I wasn't going to be another Gary Powers and spend time in a Russian prison. With what little fuel I had left I determined to get as far away as possible from that radio station. I turned left until it was directly behind me, and kept calling, "MAY DAY," until I became hoarse. With only twelve minutes of fuel left, I made a call in the clear to let anyone who might be listening know I was going off the air. A sense of despair set in as I shut down the engine.

Here I was, 75,000 feet above who knows where, encased in a pressure suit which had inflated to keep my blood from boiling and all I could think of was what a fine mess I'd gotten myself into this time. When the suit inflated, I neglected to pull the lanyard that keeps the helmet from rising and had a hard time seeing the instrument panel until I finally got it back in place. The windshield fogged up immediately and the face plate fogged up shortly thereafter. I wanted to conserve the battery so I could make one call before I punched out.

For a while I thought that the altimeter had stuck. A full ten minutes went by before the aircraft started to descend. In order to see the instrument panel I had to press my helmet as close to my face as possible to be able to lick the condensation off of the face plate. Now all I had to do was keep the wings level, maintain a rate of descent for maximum range, and hope that my guardian angel wasn't taking a nap.

The silence was deafening. All that I could hear was my own labored breathing. I hadn't felt the need to relieve my bladder… until now. I wasn't about to unzip my pressure suit and risk having my penis pinched off, and besides that, I wasn't confident that I could find it under all the winter gear I was wearing anyway. I felt like how a forty pound robin must look.

I wandered off the heading I had established, not that it mattered much. It had been twenty minutes since the flame out and I'll be damned if I didn't see a faint glow on the horizon directly in front of me. I planned to hold this heading and rate of descent until I reached 20,000 feet. If I'm in an overcast, then I'd better punch out because I didn't want to hit a mountain, if indeed one was in my flight path. If it's clear, then I'll descend to 15,000 and take it from there.

As I descended through 25,000 feet, there was no cloud cover, and the pressure suit began deflating. It was now light enough to see the snow covered terrain with no mountains in sight. And I could see the two F-102s that were on each wing! They were both flying at near stall speed and their angle of attack looked dangerously steep. I actuated the battery switch and gave them a call on the emergency frequency.

They welcomed me home and said they'd been following me for the past fifteen minutes and added that I had just passed a little airstrip twenty miles back. I told the F-102 driver on my left wing I was going to make a left turn, so he'd better move out. He said, "No sweat, come on." When I turned into him, he stalled out and disappeared under my left wing. He called and said, "While I'm down here, I'll look for that little air strip."

I arrived over the strip at 20,000 feet, but couldn't make it out. All I could see were a few small shacks and the bubble of a radar station. Finally someone in one of the shacks came up on the frequency and I asked him where the runway was located. He asked if I could see the shoreline of the Chukchi Sea. The Chukchi Sea was frozen over, but I could see where the ice met land. He then told me the runway paralleled the shoreline in a north south direction. I asked where the south threshold was located. He responded by saying he would park a truck on it. I was about to tell him not to park a truck on it, but park beside it fifty feet away. No answer, he went off the air. What a ding bat!

I was down to 12,000 feet, and sure enough, I saw a truck racing toward the shoreline and then turn south. It travelled about a thousand feet before it stopped and someone jumped out waving their arms. Good… now I see where the threshold is, now move the damn truck!

At 10,000 feet I made an air start and was relieved to hear the J-57 come to life. Now I could lower the landing gear and extend the speed brakes. I continued circling, looking for a wind sock or something to indicate wind direction, but there was nothing in sight.

The U-2 is not an east aircraft to land in a direct crosswind. One of the F-102 drivers gave me an altimeter setting so all I had to do was set up a flame out pattern at 1,000 feet, miss a truck parked on the threshold, and hope for no crosswind. The F-102 drivers were getting nervous as I descended below 5,000 feet; they were used to setting up a flame out pattern with a high key of 10,000 feet… but they weren't flying a glider.

When I reached 1,000 feet above the truck I couldn't detect any crosswind, which was a big relief. I started a left turn out to sea which caused the F-102 drivers to come unglued. They called, "Bail out! Bail out! To which I replied, "Hush." I continued my turn on around to low key, lowered the flaps, and decided I was getting too much thrust out of the idling J-57, so I shut it down.

Everything looked good, but I was coming up on the truck with more airspeed than I wanted. As I passed over the truck at 15 feet, I deployed the drag chute and kicked the rudder back and forth. That took care of the excessive airspeed nicely. The U-2 didn't want to stop flying… even without an engine.

Call it luck, but I think I made my best touchdown to date. I hardly felt anything as both landing gear settled in one foot of snow. The landing roll was less than 200 feet thanks to the snow piling up in front of the landing gear. When I came to a complete stop, I just sat there staring straight ahead as if in a trance.

I was both physically and emotionally drained. I don't recall how long I sat there, but it was until a knock on the canopy startled me to attention. I turned to face a bearded giant who was grinning from ear to ear. He wore a government issue parka and very much resembled Grizzly Adams.

Before I opened the canopy I unstrapped the seat belt and shoulder harness, made sure that all the switches were off and stowed all of the useless maps. I removed the face plate and breathed real air.

After I opened the canopy the bearded giant said, "Welcome to Kotzebue." I said, "You don't know how glad I am to be here!" It was painfully cold as I tried to climb out of the cockpit with all the heavy flight gear. I didn't think my legs would support my weight… they were numb. My new found friend sensed the difficulty I was having, so he put his hands under my armpits and gently lifted me out of the cockpit and placed me on the snow. It was no effort at all for him and he wasn't standing on a ladder or box!

Several more personnel from the radar station arrived and gathered round, plus a half dozen Eskimos who lived in the shacks that I had seen from the air. Grizzly gave me a hand taking off the helmet and told someone to put it in the truck they arrived in. The two F-102s buzzed us rocking their wings, then headed east. I made a mental note to buy those guys a drink for making the landing possible.

My bladder was about to burst, so I excused myself and shuffled to the other side of the U-2. The Eskimos followed me, but saw what I was up to and politely turned their heads. More people showed up while I was peeing until I had an audience of twenty or so.

Someone in the truck was urgently shouting at Grizzly who ran over to the truck to find out that a C-54 needed to make an emergency landing immediately. The U-2 had to be moved out of the way. Grizzly produced a stout rope that he attached to the truck bumper and the tail gear and towed the U-2 off of the strip just in time to see a C-54 make an approach with one prop feathered. It was a good thing that someone thought to move the truck that was parked at the end of the strip.

The C-54 turned out to be the Duck Butt that had been trying to steer me home. As they touched down another prop wound down. They had just enough fuel to taxi off the airstrip. Grizzly drove me over to the C-54 where we had a short reunion. I wouldn't be here if it wasn't for Duck Butt and the F-102s. I couldn't find the words to thank the Duck Butt crew enough for risking their necks to save mine. They reminded me that it's what they get paid to do.

Someone at the radar site called over the UHF radio in Grizzly's truck saying that the OL commander wanted me to call him over a secure phone. By now the F-102 drivers had notified Eielson AFB that one of their U-2s was down at Kotzebue. It was probably Whip Wilson wanting to know how the bird was.

I was glad to be inside a warm building and couldn't wait to get out of the pressure suit. The radar site commander showed me to a secure phone in his office and brought me a mug of hot coffee. Sure enough it was Lt./Col. Wilson who had been standing by the radio ever since I took off. I assured him that the aircraft suffered no damage, but the fuel tanks were dry. He advised me that a C-47 was presently loading up drums of fuel and maintenance personnel and he would be coming along to fly the U-2 back to Eielson. I asked if anyone had advised Jeanne that I was overdue, but no one had. It was good that I would be the one to tell her about my mishap. He did say my little excursion over Russia sure had the White House and SAC headquarters all shook up... I had no doubt about that.

It would be several hours before the C-47 would land at Kotzebue, so I had time to unwind and get acquainted with the radar site personnel. The site commander asked me if I'd like to see where I'd been and, of course, I did.

He took me into a room with the biggest plotting screen I had ever seen. There was a map of the polar region, which included Alaska and Siberia, about fifteen feet square overlaid with clear plastic. He flipped a switch and a battery of lights illuminated the entire screen... and there was my entire flight from start to finish indicated by little tick marks made with a yellow grease pencil.

The tick marks traced a path from Eielson AFB direct to Barter Island and direct to the North Pole. A 90 degree left turn over the pole was indicated, but instead of a 270 degree turn in the opposite direction, it looked like I turned 300 or 310 degrees before rolling out and heading for Siberia. I was beginning to seethe at this point.

I followed the tick marks where the Duck Butt navigator told me to steer 10 degrees left and later 15 degrees left. Then the tick marks made a sharp left turn and headed for

Kotzebue. I was about to ask the radar site commander why in hell I hadn't been given a steer when all along they knew where I was, but my attention focused on six little tick marks on either side of my flight path as I changed course to Kotzebue.

I asked, "What are those six little curly Qs?" He answered, "Those little curly Qs represent the six Migs that were nipping up trying to shoot you down." I said to myself, "Shit oh dear, I'm glad I didn't know that at the time... Whew!" Fearing that my legs were about to give out, I stumbled to a chair to take the weight off. He pulled up a chair alongside mine and said, "I know what you're thinking and I don't blame you. But there is a good reason why we couldn't help you. I can't tell you, but maybe some higher-up will." I responded, "Gee thanks, I hope the reason justifies throwing away an aircraft and crew."

I was still digesting all I had just learned when a phone rang. Someone in another room called out that it was for the U-2 pilot. It was one of the F-102 pilots stationed at Galena AFB, Alaska who had escorted me into Kotzebue. He was glad that I had made it down safely and apologized for yelling, "BAIL OUT," when I turned out to sea at 1,000 feet. He had never seen a U-2 and was amazed that they could glide like that. I invited him to come visit me at Eielson where I'd give him a personal tour.

The C-47 arrived from Eielson with Lt./Col. Wilson, some maintenance personnel, and enough fuel to get the U-2 back to Eielson. When Wilson checked the aircraft forms he noticed that I neglected to fill in my takeoff and landing time. I took off at midnight, but I didn't notice when I landed... I was busy. The radar site had logged me down at

1025. That's ten hours and twenty-five minutes of flight time. The U-2 has nine hours and forty minutes of fuel, so that was forty-five minutes glide time.

After Wilson took off in the U-2, I climbed aboard the C-47 with the maintenance crew for the long haul back to Eielson. Wee Willie met the C-47 and told me I had thirty minutes to pack all of my gear because there was a KC-135 waiting to fly me to SAC headquarters at Offutt AFB in Omaha, Nebraska. There I was to brief General Power (SAC commander) and his staff on my over flight of Russia.

Willie also informed me that my friend and neighbor at Laughlin, Major Rudolph Anderson, had been shot down over Cuba that day by a SA-2 surface to air missile. That bad news really knocked the wind out of my sails. He would be sorely missed by everyone who knew him.

I was hoping to get a bite to eat at Eielson, but there was no time for that. I was hoping there would be some chow on the KC-135. I don't recall how long the flight was to Offutt AFB, but it couldn't have taken long enough to suit me. I dreaded facing General Power after all that had transpired in the past twenty-four hours. I was the only passenger aboard the KC-135 which gave me an extra dose of anxiety about the briefing I would be giving at SAC headquarters. General Power must have thought it was very important to hear the circumstances surrounding my over flight from me personally. Surely he had all the details by now, but I suppose he wanted to hear it from the horse's mouth… or horse's ass.

The KC-135 flight crew were dying of curiosity about why

they were flying one guy to SAC headquarters, but they never came right out and asked. They had probably been briefed not to discuss the reason for the flight with anyone… especially me. They did provide that hot meal I was hoping for.

After landing at Offutt, I was met by a staff car that took me to SAC headquarters where I was met by a full Colonel who escorted me to the underground command post. The place was a beehive of activity with people literally running from place to place as if their lives depended on it.

Adjacent to the command post was a large briefing room with a large table that could accommodate at least twenty people. At the head of the table stood an easel that held an aeronautical chart on which my flight to the North Pole was plotted. A sheet of paper was taped over the portion of the chart that depicted my flight after leaving the Pole. The Colonel told me to take a seat and Gen. Power would be with us in a few minutes.

Gen. Power entered the room followed by eight other Generals who looked as if they had slept in their uniforms for days. Their eyes were bloodshot and they all hadn't seen a razor in at least 24 hours. I stood at attention until they all were seated. Gen. Power sat directly across the table from me and was the only person in the room I recognized.

As soon as everyone was seated, with their eyes riveted on me, Gen. Power said, "Captain Maultsby, how about briefing us on your flight yesterday." I stood at the easel while describing the type of mission, then took a pointer and indicated the route flown from Eielson to the North

Pole. I mentioned the difficulty taking fixes because of the Aurora Borealis. No one stopped me to ask questions until I pointed to the North Pole.

Gen. Power then asked, "Captain Maultsby, do you know where you went after leaving the Pole?" I answered, "Yes sir." The other generals squirmed in their seats as if they were sitting on tacks. Gen. Power then said, "Show us please."

I lifted the paper that covered my flight path after leaving the Pole. The other generals really became excited at that point, but Gen. Power merely smiled and asked, "How did you know?" I told him I was shown my flight path plotted on the big screen back at the radar site.

Gen. Power then turned and looked from one general to another and asked, "Gentlemen, do you have any questions?" They all nodded negative. He then looked back at me and said, "Too bad you weren't configured with a system to gather electromagnetic radiation. The Russians probably had every radar and ICBM (intercontinental ballistic missile) site on maximum alert."

Gen. Power thanked me for the briefing, ordered me not to discuss my over flight with anyone, and left the room. The other generals followed in order of rank. The last to leave the room was a Brigadier General who stopped and said to me, "You are a lucky sonofabitch. I've seen Gen. Power chew up and spit out people for doing a hellova lot less."

The Colonel who escorted me into the command post asked if I'd like to wait in his office for the U-3A that was flying up from Laughlin to pick me up. It wasn't due for over an hour, so I thought this would be a good time to find out why I wasn't given a steer when every Tom, Dick and Harry all had my flight path plotted. The Colonel wouldn't say why I wasn't given a steer, but he did offer that my over flight came very close to starting World War III. If it hadn't been for my 'May Day' calls, the Russians probably would have pulled the trigger! He also told me when President Kennedy was informed about my over flight he simply said, "There's always some sonofabitch that doesn't get the word." ...Well... I wished that sonofabitch had been sitting on my lap! If I'd gotten the word, like simply a steer, I wouldn't be sitting here. Just one steer would have prevented all of this commotion.

A phone call from Base Ops announced the arrival of a U-3A from Laughlin. I thanked the Colonel for his hospitality and left still wondering why I wasn't given a steer. It would bug me for months before I found out why.

Capt. Ed Perdue was waiting for me in the flight planning room. He told me everyone back at Laughlin had been extremely concerned, but he didn't think anyone had said anything to Jeanne... for which I was thankful. He was anxious to hear all about my fiasco, but didn't pursue the issue after I told him about my order from Gen. Power not to discuss it.

Ed said he'd flown through some pretty nasty weather on the way up and hoped it had cleared for the flight back. The weather station forecast was not optimistic.

Just north of Enid, Oklahoma we ran into icing conditions and couldn't maintain altitude. We called Vance AFB, located near Enid, to inform them we were icing up and requested immediate landing instructions. Making matters worse, one of the engines was losing power which increased our rate of descent. We requested a straight in GCA (ground controlled approach) and declared an emergency. When the GCA picked us up we were already below the glide path still descending. This would be a hellova way to go after all that I'd been through the past two days.

GCA was screaming at us to level off, we were way below the glide path. I could see the ground now and was certain that that we wouldn't make it to the runway that was barely visible through light fog. I swear Ed was trying to hold the airplane up by pulling up on the yoke. It worked because we touched down on the overrun fifty feet from the runway.

Two emergency landings in as many days was more than I bargained for when I fought so hard for those silver wings eleven years ago.

The remainder of the flight to Laughlin was uneventful. We were met by a staff car that took us to the command post where the Wing Commander, Col. Des Portes, and his staff were waiting to hear my version of the Russian over flight; and my briefing with Gen. Power. Everyone was disappointed that I was under orders not to discuss the matter. Col. Des Portes simply said, "Go home Chuck."

Jeanne was shocked to see me walk in the house with all of my luggage. Chuckie and Shawn weren't home to ask me, "What did you bring me?" It was their standard greeting whenever I came home from a long absence. After a big hug and kiss, Jeanne asked me what had happened and offered that I looked like I hadn't slept in a week. I told her I'd tell her the whole story after a shower and a change into something comfortable.

As I stepped out of the shower the phone rang. Jeanne answered it and called out to me that Col. Des Portes wanted me to come to the Command post ASAP, if not sooner. Thank goodness I had some clean uniforms in the closet because the one I'd just shed was still standing where I left it.

It was only a few minutes' drive from our house to Wing Headquarters, but a zillion thoughts flashed through my mind during that few minutes. What the hell was so important that it couldn't wait another hour or two?

When I entered the command post, almost every officer in the Wing was assembled. It was standing room only and Col. Des Portes was seated at a table much like the one in the SAC command post. He asked me to take the seat opposite him. I noticed an easel depicting my now infamous flight standing next to me.

Col. Des Portes began by stating, "Chuck, when General Power ordered you not to discuss your flight with anyone, he didn't mean not to discuss it with us. He complimented you for strictly following his orders."

You could hear a pin drop for the next two hours as I gave my detailed briefing. There were a couple of muttered, "Oh shits," as I described the six Migs after my fanny, but no one asked a question until I finished. Everyone was more interested in my thoughts during the ordeal than the cause of it. Everyone expressed relief that they weren't in my shoes.

With that, Col. Des Portes thanked me and added, "Now get back to Jeanne and the boys and take the next two days off."

Jeanne met me at the door with a cool one and a question, "Does all this have anything to do with Rudolph Anderson being shot down?" The Andersons lived two doors down and we'd become good friends. I told her I'd tell the whole story after I changed, and no, it had nothing to do with Rudolph. I also mentioned that if the boys came home during my story we'd have to wait until we were alone again to continue.

Jeanne sat as still as a mouse, with her huge eyes looking even larger, as I related the events of the last three days. When I finished she just shook her head and said, "I let you out of my sight for an instant and you try to start World War Three!"

At that instant Chuckie and Shawn burst through the door shouting, "What did you bring me?" I felt like saying, "I brought your Daddy's ass home in one piece, that's what I brought you!" …but I didn't. All the commotion woke up Little Kevin who had grown during the time I was away. He strongly voiced his displeasure at being disturbed.

SAC Headquarters sent a team of navigators down to Laughlin to get a look at the article known as the U-2. Most had never seen one, nor the navigation aids it carried. The team leader was a full colonel who, upon meeting me, mentioned that he remembered my name being associated with another incident, but couldn't put his finger on it.

I was chosen to escort the team because they were well aware of my over flight of Russia. I had them take turns sitting in the cockpit as I explained what this and that was and how it was operated. I think they were all expecting to see all sorts of sophisticated equipment and seemed disappointed at what they saw. Most shared a sentiment expressed by one fellow who said, "I wouldn't try to navigate this thing around the block, much less around the world!"

After several days of observing the flight planning and results of the flight, they all agreed that a U-2 pilot definitely earned his flight pay.

As the team was departing for SAC Headquarters, the Colonel called me aside and said he remembered where he'd heard my name before. He'd been on duty in the SAC command post last July 4th, when all hell broke loose. In spite of the tight security a group of saboteurs had infiltrated Laughlin AFB. The highest state of alert was sent from Laughlin to SAC Headquarters. When all of the dust settled, the group of saboteurs turned out to be Captain Maultsby, Major Loden and their families.

I remembered the incident only too well. The boys and I loved to set off fireworks on the 4th of July. We always picked some spot to do it where the likelihood of starting a fire was low. The Laughlin skeet range would do nicely as there was no vegetation to ignite.

Around 2100, the Loden's and Maultsby's all piled into their cars and drove the mile to the skeet range. We first fired off a couple of large skyrockets to start the show, but after no more than a minute we found ourselves confronted by a weapons carrier armed with a 50 caliber machine gun pointed directly at us and four armed guards holding leashes that prevented the K-9s from tearing us to pieces!

Bright spot lights illuminated our terrified little group and some of the younger kids started crying. The sergeant in charge approached me and asked for my ID. He then called the command post and reported that a Captain Maultsby, a Major Loden, and their families were shooting off fireworks at the skeet range. I heard the voice over the radio respond by saying, "Aww shit!... I already alerted SAC!"

After advising us to go home, the sergeant, guards, K-9s and the weapons carrier all disappeared as quickly and as quietly as it had appeared.

The next morning the chief of the command post gave me a thorough briefing on security procedures and pointed out that firing off flares or rockets on a high a high security base was not a good idea… ever. He finished by saying, "And Chuck, SAC Headquarters ordered me to order you to go play somewhere else next 4th of July."

I spent November and December of 1962, and January of 1963, flying missions out of Laughlin and McCoy AFB, Florida. These included thirteen missions over Cuba photographing missile sites that were definitely active. On several occasions the missile sites would go to launch mode, which was indicated by a sensor in the cockpit. Looking through the drift sight for signs of a missile firing was disconcerting to say the least. Thank God no missiles were ever fired at me, but I did see Migs several thousand feet below me on several missions.

I never saw the results of my missions because the film was downloaded from the Q-bay as soon as the aircraft came to a complete stop. It was then loaded on a transport plane and flown to a photo lab in Washington D.C. The film was on its way before I could get out of the cockpit.

One mission that I flew on January 19th, 1963, evidently produced some significant results because I was awarded the Distinguished Flying Cross. The citation read:

Captain Charles W. Maultsby distinguished himself by extraordinary achievement while participating in aerial flight as an aircraft commander, 4028th Strategic Reconnaissance Weather Squadron, 4080th Strategic Wing, Strategic Air Command on 19 January 1963. On that date, Captain Maultsby successfully completed a mission of grave national interest and international significance by piloting an unarmed aircraft over hostile target areas to obtain information of vital importance to the security of the United States. The professional competence, aerial skill and devotion to duty displayed by Captain Maultsby reflect great credit to himself and the United States Air Force.

Notice the aircraft was not identified as a U-2, or that the target areas were Cuban missile sites.

One evening in March of 1963, Jeanne and I were watching TV when the phone rang about 2200 hours. It was Marty, an agency U-2 pilot who I met before, telling me to get over to the Officers Club right away. I told him I wasn't dressed and invited him over to the house. He yelled back, "Chuck! Get your ass over here NOW!"… and hung up. Jeanne asked what that was all about. I told her, "I don't know, but I'm going to find out."

When I entered the club, Marty and three other fellas in civilian attire were standing at the bar. They were the only ones there and even the bartender was absent. Marty signaled me over and announced, "Gentlemen, this is Captain Maultsby." I shook each of their hands, but none of the three offered his name. I thought it was peculiar, but I took it in stride.

We stood around chatting idly for ten minutes then abruptly the three said goodnight and left. I thought to myself, "Those guys would make first rate undertakers." I turned to Marty and asked, "What the hell is going on? You got me over here for this? He answered, "Calm down Chuck, those three gentlemen are from the agency and came down to size you up. You may hear from them again." With that said, Marty walked off without another word, leaving me standing alone in the empty club.

When I told Jeanne what took place, she said, "Well, if you do hear back from them, that'll be great; it's what you wanted in the first place… I certainly won't complain about a nice raise in pay."

Word got around that the 4080th Wing was going to move to Davis-Monthan AFB in Tucson, Arizona during the coming summer. Air Training Command was moving an Undergraduate Pilot Training Wing to Laughlin. I can't say I didn't enjoy our stay in Del Rio, but personally, I would savor the move.

An alert lady in the Education Office called me sometime in April, 1963. She'd been reviewing my education records and noticed that I didn't have enough credits toward a degree in aeronautical engineering; and I qualified for

Operation Bootstrap (Air Force Educational Leave of Absence Program). She'd already taken the liberty to contact Northrop Institute of Technology and inquire about what subjects I needed to receive a degree. I needed a course in statistics, economics, chemistry and chemistry lab. I had already completed the math and science courses when I went to Northrop from 1946 to 1948. She told me I could enroll in September.

Jeanne was all for living near her family while I went to Northrop, the boys would love the beach and all of the L.A. attractions, so we decided to give it a go. Besides, a degree on your service record looks good to a promotion board.

The wing 'weenies' weren't too happy about letting a qualified U-2 pilot go off to school for nine months, but they reluctantly approved my request. However… they did schedule me to go TDY to our OL in Australia in June for three months.

The Wing move coincided with my departure to Australia so I moved Jeanne and the boys to Hawthorne, California to await my return. Jeanne's parents lived a few blocks from the house we rented which was close to Northrop. Her sister's family lived in Redondo Beach, her brother's family lived in West Covina, so she would have plenty of company for the next three months.

Jeanne and the boys saw me off at LAX for a flight to Tucson, where I would meet up with the detachment going to Australia. Saying goodbye doesn't get any easier no matter how many times you have to say it. Jeanne never complained, although I'm sure she would have preferred that I work a 9 to 5 at home. Being an Air Force wife does have its disadvantages.

As the aircraft taxied away from the terminal, I recalled leaving Jeanne and little Chuckie like this twelve years before. Well, little Chuckie was twelve years old now and would be a big help to his mother.

Lt./Col. Leatherwood was the OL commander. Capt. Dave Ray and I would replace the pilots at the RAAF Laverton airfield. I considered Australia to be the choice OL assignment, but I would much rather be going there in the summer months. I heard that the winter is cold and overcast nine-tenths of the time. Shades of Alaska during their winter months.

The flight to Australia aboard a C-135 was long and uneventful. We made refueling stops in Hawaii and the Fiji Islands, but had no time for any sightseeing. Upon our arrival at Laverton, we were met by the U-2 drivers who couldn't wait to be homeward bound.

Several RAAF types were on hand to welcome us. It was customary for the incoming and outgoing OL personnel to be hosted to a formal dining-in by the Wing Commander or Group Leader. An RAAF group leader is the equivalent of a full colonel in our Air Force. The dining-in was scheduled for the next evening. If I'd known what was in store for me, I probably would have gone AWOL (absent without leave).

We were quartered in the Officers Mess which was a huge brick edifice without central heating. The ceiling throughout were twenty feet high. There was a single fireplace located in the bar, but what little heat emanated from the fireplace quickly rose to the ceiling.

The few RAAF types that I met, prior to the dining-in, went out of their way to make us newcomers feel at home. But I had a feeling that they knew more about me than what they could have gleaned from the pilots we were replacing.

The dining-in was scheduled for 1800 hours and everyone was expected to be in place when the Group Leader entered. He was the spit and polish type who reminded me of the movie actor Sir Cedric Hardwicke. The dining hall could accommodate about sixty people seated around a 'U' shaped table. Name tags had been placed in order of rank making sure that no two Americans sat together.

One of my dinner partners was Chaplin O'Regan who was a hellova nice guy with whom I would spend many off-duty hours seeing the sights of Melbourne and attending Australian style football games.

We were all standing behind our chairs when, promptly at 1800 hours, the Group leader entered and asked us to be seated. He remained standing and waited for everybody to be seated. He then began a speech bidding the departing OL members a hail and farewell. Next he introduced the replacement team beginning with Lt./Col. Leatherwood.

When my turn came to be introduced, the Group Leader hesitated a few moments. I noticed everyone looking at me with a shit-eaten grin on their faces. Satisfied that his pause had produced the desired effect he began, "There may be a few among you who have not met Captain

Maultsby personally, but you certainly know him by reputation." Oh God, I then knew what was coming.

For the benefit of the few who had not heard the story about me being the bugger who wiped a booger on the RAAF Chief of Staff, the Group Leader took great delight in repeating it exactly as it happened. After he'd finished everyone clapped and stomped their feet with great enthusiasm. I wanted to slide under the table out of embarrassment.

For the next three months not one RAAF personnel ever offered to shake my hand.

I only flew nine missions during the three month tour; the same boring high altitude air sampling that I'd done in Alaska. If it hadn't been for the friendliness of every Aussie we met, the three months could have been beyond monotonous.

At first I thought the friendliness was somewhat exaggerated, which prompted me to ask Chaplain O'Regan why the Aussies evidently held the Yanks in such high esteem. He told me that every man, woman and child knew that if it wasn't for the Yanks, the Japanese would have invaded Australia… and they will never forget it. It didn't matter that none of us had anything to do with preventing an invasion; we were Yanks, and that was all that mattered. It was common for an Aussie civilian to show up at the Officers Mess and ask if there were any Yanks about. Dave and I were often taken into their homes for a hearty meal and pleasant conversation. The children were especially in awe of the pilots who flew the strange looking aircraft.

On a dozen occasions Dave and I were invited to visit schools to conduct question and answer sessions. The kids were mostly interested in life in the United States and seemed to think that America was the land of milk and honey where everyone was rich. Trying to convince them otherwise was fruitless.

We were impressed with how the children conducted themselves at every school. They obviously received the same discipline at home and school. They attended school year round without summer vacation.

The RAAF is a rather small outfit compared to ours, so I thought looking up my old Aussie POW buddy, Butch Hanna, wouldn't be difficult. Chaplain O'Regan offered to inquire around and put the word out that I'd spent time as a POW with Butch.

In a few days I was contacted by an Aussie F-86 pilot who informed me that Butch had been killed only two years after coming home. He'd been an instructor pilot at the local training base. He added that Butch's Grandmother lived in Melbourne and would like to meet me.

I had misgivings about meeting her fearing that old wounds might be reopened, but I worried for nothing. We met and she adopted me and the F-86 jock as if we were family. We spent several Sundays together and became good friends; she insisted that I call her 'Nanny.' She never mentioned Butch… nor did I.

By the end of my tour I was convinced that if I ever had to live somewhere other than the good ole USA, it would be Australia. Our departure was celebrated the same as our arrival had been; a dining-in to welcome our replacements and bid farewell to us. I'll never forget the many friends I made and the kindness of the Australian people.

The flight home aboard a C-135 seemed to take longer than the flight to Australia. Three months away from loved ones can be an eternity. I was now determined to get out of this U-2 business and lead a normal nine to five existence. At least for the next nine months I'd be home every night.

Upon arriving at Davis-Monthan AFB on September 17th, I received orders to attend 'Operation Bootstrap.' Classes began on September 30th, so I would have until then to become reacquainted with my family. I was on a plane headed for L.A. on the 18th.

Jeanne and the boys met me at LAX where I was bombarded by questions such as, "Did ya see any kangaroos?", "Did ya bring us a Koala Bear?", "Why is it winter in Australia?", and "Does the toilet water really go backwards?" There were more questions all the way home. I don't think the boys missed me at all. They kept Jeanne going from sunup to sundown to places like Disneyland, Marineland, Knott's Berry Farm and the beach.

In order to receive flight pay I was assigned to HQ 6592nd Support Group, Space Systems Division, located at LAX flying the same ole U-3A 'Bug Smasher.' There were many other officer-pilots like myself attending USC, UCLA or Northrop to finish their degrees. Flying time became a scarce commodity.

Getting back into the academic harness was an eye opener. My study habits had long since deserted me; on top of taking courses I couldn't have cared less about to get a degree that I would never use. However, I managed to get fair grades, completed the degree requirements, and graduated on June 21st, 1964. Nine months prior to June 21st I couldn't even spell Aeronautical Engineer... and now I are one!

Tragedy struck twice in November during my college year. On November 20th, I got a phone call from a fellow U-2 pilot, Captain Cliff Beeler, who informed me that our good friend, Joe Hyde, had been killed during a U-2 mission off the Southern tip of Florida after egressing Cuba.

Two days later I was working on a project in the chemistry lab when our professor entered and announced that President Kennedy had been assassinated. School was closed immediately and everyone went straight home to follow the developments on TV. Jeanne was glued to the TV set when I got home. We didn't turn it off for the next two and a half days.

There were good times too during my schooling at Northrop. Jeanne and I received tickets to the Rose Bowl in a Christmas card from a friend. We enjoyed watching Illinois beat Washington 17 to 7. Then on February 27th, 1964, I was promoted to Major.

A few days after my promotion, Marty, the agency U-2 pilot dropped by the house to inform me that I had been selected to become 'one of the boys.' The catch was... I would have to leave immediately.

Well, this was out of the question. Those who went to school under 'Operation Bootstrap' either completed their courses, or were castrated… or some similar fate. I wondered why they couldn't have waited until June.

When I had to pass on the offer, the agency selected two other pilots from the squadron. The promotion to Major helped ease the pain of having to give up the money I'd have gotten as an agency U-2 driver, but it didn't come close to matching it.

Chuckie and some of his friends at school were very much into surfing and trying to organize a band after seeing "The Beatles" on the Ed Sullivan show. "The Beach Boys" had grown up in our present neighborhood and could often be seen visiting their parent's house a block away, which was further inspiration for Chuckie and his fledgling band mates. He badgered me to buy him a surfboard and a guitar until I finally relented. I bought a surfboard kit and spent countless hours putting it together in the garage. I also bought him a Sears *Silvertone* electric guitar. Little did we, or he, know then that the guitar would launch him on a career that he's pursued to this day. He's a professional singer and songwriter with his own band called, "Chuck Wagon and the Wheels," who are based in Tucson, Arizona.

The boys weren't happy about having to leave California for another bout with the desert. The shock was lessened somewhat when we found a nice off-base house with a pool. The boy's schools were nearby and they had built-in friends who had transferred from Laughlin a year before. Our pool was constantly in use that first summer in Tucson.

As for me, it was back to the U-2 business as usual. I was

just about resigned to the fact that I'd never get back into fighters when fate intervened. In April of 1965, the chief of the Quality Control Board, Major Boyd, was transferred to another outfit. I volunteered to replace him immediately knowing full well that I would no longer have a crew number nor any more TDYs or OLs. Because I had the Aeronautical Engineering degree, and the fact that I had over 900 hours in the U-2, I was selected as his replacement. If Major Boyd could be reassigned, then why not me?

In the meantime, being the chief of the Quality Control Board would be about as close to a nine to five job as you can have in the military. Jeanne could now plan a meal and expect me to be there for it.

As chief of the Quality Control Branch, my duties were less than stressful. Other than supervising eight NCOs, who were experts in their fields and needed no supervision, I flew all the test flights in the U-2 and T-33. Whenever maintenance was performed on either aircraft I took it up to determine if it could fulfill its mission. Very seldom did I have occasion to write up a discrepancy; the maintenance was that good.

It was customary for every officer in the Air Force to check his personnel folder, at one time or another, located at Randolph AFB in San Antonio, Texas. Most officers checked their folder if they were due for a promotion to insure they were up to date, etc. I wasn't due for promotion, but I decided to tag along with another U-2 driver that was. I had no test flights scheduled, so we took off in a T-33 early one early morning figuring we could make it back the same day.

While strolling through the halls of the Air Force Military Personnel Center, someone came up from behind me and shouted, "Chuck Maultsby, what in hell are you doing here?" Much to my surprise it was Major Bill Callahan who I hadn't seen since our stay at March Field when we were repatriated. He first reminded me of the time we almost got thrown out of the Officers Club for singing a song that belittled bomber jocks. When I told Bill I was there to check my personnel folder, he invited me to follow him to his office. On his office door was a sign that read:

OFFICER ASSIGNMENT BRANCH

Bill called the office where my folder was kept and had it delivered to his office. We spent an hour reviewing the pile of papers when Bill finally asked, "What possessed you to join the U-2 outfit?"

I told him the whole story while he just nodded his head from side to side in disbelief. Finally I said, "There you have it Bill, my quest for gold turned to lead." He offered that he'd seen some mighty queer shenanigans take place since being assigned to personnel, but my story takes the cake. Bill excused himself and went into another room. When he returned, he was thumbing through several documents.

When he was finished reading whatever it was he asked, "How would you like to get back into fighters?" Before I could answer he added, "I can't promise you anything because SAC will scream like a wounded AP if we reassign one of their own, but the need for fighter pilots in SEA (Southeast Asia) is critical. You might be facing a tour in SEA if I got you back in fighters. And since there's an F-4 RTU (Replacement Training Unit) stationed at Davis-Monthan, it's likely that you would check out in the F-4."

I couldn't believe what I was hearing! Checking out in an F-4 exceeded my wildest dreams. Many times, as I taxied past row after row of F-4s in a U-2, I thought about what I'd give to get into one of those. My head was spinning with the possibility. Bill could see how excited I was and again cautioned me not to get my hopes up too high. SAC would put up a fight, but they don't always win. The last thing Bill said was, "I'll do what I can Chuck, but keep this under your hat until you hear from me."

*   *   *

Chapter 10

Vietnam

Jeanne took the news about the possibility of my getting back into fighters with much skepticism. She didn't like the idea of me going to Vietnam for who knows how long with the possibility of my becoming a POW again... or worse. I tried to placate her by saying there was no guarantee that I would be reassigned, but she wouldn't buy it.

She could understand Korea because I entered pilot training before that fracas started, but Vietnam was another story. She knew what Major Grady Morris, a squadron commander at Nellis who had recently returned from Vietnam, said about it not being worth the bother to go over there because of all the flying restrictions. I found it difficult to believe Major Morris, but he was a straight shooter in every way and not a man to be taken lightly.

I really didn't think I had a snowball's chance in hell of getting back into fighters. SAC would see to that. Besides that, I was feeling guilty about only thinking of myself when I had a wife and three kids who had tolerated my long absences without complaint.

Jeanne was right, why not relax and enjoy the cushy job with no TDYs and the guarantee of being home every night. At least, where I was, I could do some loops, spins and rolls in the T-33 when no one was looking. SAC frowned on such maneuvers. I was appalled to learn that none of the U-2 jocks had ever spun in a T-33, or any other aircraft for that matter. I had been asked to do a little clandestine instructing; but flirting with a court martial discouraged that.

I was just beginning to enjoy my nine to five lifestyle, including a dip in the pool each night before dinner, when I received a phone call in late July. I received orders to go TDY to the 4453rd Combat Crew Training Wing at Davis Monthan AFB for the purpose of attending the F-4C USAF Operational Training Course 111509F. Length of course, sixteen weeks. Reporting date, 7 August, 1966. Upon completion of TDY, I was to report to the 558 Tactical Fighter Squadron, PACAF (Pacific Air Force) APO San Francisco, California 96326.

Not only were the 'Wing Weenies' ticked off, Jeanne was seeing red! She had taken all of my absences in stride, but this was the straw that could break the camel's back. Unlike the Korean fracas, where you could fly 100 missions and return home, there was no assurance that you could do that in Vietnam. A tour in Vietnam could last up to twelve months, and she knew it.

The 558 Tactical Fighter Squadron was stationed at Cam Ranh Bay located on the southeast coast of Vietnam and a long way from Hanoi. One hundred missions flown in North Vietnam was a ticket home, but most of the missions north were flown by units in Ubon and Udorn, Thailand and Da Nang, Vietnam. Inflight refueling was necessary in order for units at Cam Ranh to reach Hanoi. So most of the missions flown by the 558th would be 'in country,' or in the south. Well, maybe things would change over there by the time I checked out in the F-4C.

My immediate supervisor, a full colonel in the U-2 outfit, was very put out with me for going behind his back by requesting a transfer. He grew up in SAC and couldn't understand why anyone would want to fly fighters and said so in my efficiency report.

I called Bill at the Air Force Military Personnel Center and thanked him for what he had done for me. He said he was glad to do a fellow fighter pilot a favor, but it was not without a knock down drag out fight with SAC. He advised me to be invisible for the next sixteen weeks because he hadn't heard the last from SAC.

I was assigned to the 4456th Combat Crew Training Squadron, class 67 BRD where I met some of the instructors I served with at Nellis. It was like old home week. There were sixteen aircraft commanders and sixteen Weapon Systems Operators (WSO) in our class. The WSOs or GIB (guy in back) were fresh out of pilot training and didn't relish the thought of flying in the back seat. I couldn't blame them, but after a tour in SEA they would upgrade to aircraft commander.

My GIB was Lt. Tommy B. Almquist, one of the finest young men I've ever known. Although Tommy would much rather have been flying the front seat, he never complained and quickly learned his duties as a WSO. I was sorry to learn that we wouldn't be going to SEA together. He was slated for a unit at Da Nang.

The next sixteen weeks were like a vacation. Fly half a day, ground school the other half, and home by 1700 hours. It was nice being on the other end of the stick. Someone else did the scheduling, briefings, debriefings and all the other things it takes to turn out a combat crew. God knows I did enough of it at Nellis.

My first flight in the F-4C took place on the 24th of August, 1966. My instructor was Captain Bill Patton. Just looking at an F-4C on the ground makes you wonder how anything so big and ugly can flit like a butterfly once it's airborne. The first time I saw one, it reminded me of a tank with wings. But just one flight in an F-4 is all it takes to hunger for more. It's the most stable gunnery platform I had flown to date and could reach speeds exceeding twice the speed of sound.

Things were going smoothly for the first four weeks of training when lo and behold, two more of SACs U-2 jocks managed to escape their surly bonds and reported for Combat Crew Training in the F-4C. How Majors Ted Baader and Jim Qualls pulled it off I don't know, but Bill didn't have a hand in it.

The three of us were summoned to the F-4 Wing Headquarters for a chat with Colonel Chappie James (later to become the first African American four star general) who was the director of Operations (DO).

He advised us that SAC was raising all kinds of hell, just short of accusing him of unethical recruiting practices. He said it was getting so bad that he doubted if any of us would get to complete our training. He didn't ask us how we managed to escape SAC, but he did caution us to lie low and not make any waves... And avoid visiting our friends still in the U-2s... enough said.

Tommy and I flew a total of forty-eight sorties in the F-4 during the sixteen week course. We were a good team and I was sorry to see him go to another outfit when we completed training. He was as sharp as they come. Being a bachelor, Tommy spent many evenings at our house for dinner, then playing with the boys and their pets. We knew he was having bouts of homesickness, so we tried to make him feel at home as possible.

The sixteen weeks seemed to fly by (no pun intended) and another goodbye was forthcoming. Jeanne has never forgiven me for exposing myself to another tour of combat; leaving her with the responsibility of raising three boys and not knowing from day to day whether or not she would be receiving a telegram like the one she received fourteen years earlier.

There were too many telegrams being delivered around Tucson in those days. Many of the wives whose husbands had completed training at Davis-Monthan elected to remain in Tucson until their husbands returned from Vietnam. Too many husbands never returned.

Jeanne and the boys saw me off in mid-December at the

Tucson International Airport. I was going off to war in a commercial airliner... what was the military coming to? I do admit that it was better than the old C-54 I made the trip in during August of 1951.

Captain Dick Vogel was my traveling companion all the way to the Philippines. He was in the same class as me, 67BRD, but was assigned to a unit in Ubon, Thailand. It was the last time I'd see him until 1973. He was shot down over Hanoi and spent the duration as a POW in the Hanoi Hilton.

All incoming crews were supposed to remain in the Philippines to undergo Jungle Survival Training before reporting to their unit in Vietnam. I knew how important this type of training was, but couldn't see hanging around the Philippines for two or three weeks.

I hitched a ride on a C-130 headed for Cam Ranh Bay, home of the 12th Tactical Fighter Wing. Upon arriving, I went directly to Wing Headquarters and gained an audience with the wing director of operations, Col. Travis McNeil. He was expecting me and gave me a thumbnail sketch of the wing's mission.

After introducing me to the Wing Commander, Col. Woodard Davis, Col. McNeil told me that I wouldn't be going to the 558th Squadron. I'd be going to the 557th Squadron instead as the Assistant Operations Officer. At the time it didn't matter to me where I went, but as it turned out, I really lucked out!

I immediately could tell that the 557th Squadron Commander, Lt/Col. William Adams, and his Operations

Officer, Lt/Col. William Fuller, would be a pleasure to work for. I was also pleased to see that some of the aircraft commanders were former students of mine. I had checked them out in the F-86 and F-100 back at Nellis. It really is a small world.

Lt./Col. Fuller told me to spend the rest of the day getting settled in and tomorrow he'd go over my duties with me and schedule an in-country briefing, better known as 'the rules of engagement.' My quarters were a trailer I was to share with Majors Tom Normile and Charlie Rhymes. We soon became the best of friends and earned a reputation for being the best scroungers in the Wing.

I was pleasantly surprised to find all the facilities on base to be first rate, especially the mess hall. It was all as good as stateside. Commercial airlines shared the base with us; the airline terminal was located across the field from us. True to his word, Lt./Col. Fuller went over my duties with me the next day.

They were: Supervise all squadron flying activities. Co-ordinate programming and scheduling of aircraft and crews. Responsible for squadron flight management, standardization and operational status. Advise the operations officer in all areas of tactical fighter operations and employment. Supervise all flight commanders, aircrews and administrative personnel. Direct planning and execution of all operational plans in a combat environment. Perform duty as an Instructor Pilot. And last, but not least, fly as many combat missions as time permits. It sounded like a pretty tall order, but I intended to have plenty of help.

Next on the agenda was the in-country briefing for all the new heads. The Wing Intelligence Officer usually gave the briefing, but on this occasion it was given by a visiting Seventh Air Force staff officer. There were about ten of us attending the briefing to learn what we could and couldn't do while carrying out a combat mission. 'Rules of engagement' it was called.

Well, this staff officer prefaced his briefing by saying, "Gentlemen, there isn't a target over here worth an aircraft or crew." I couldn't help but retort, "Then what the hell are we doing over here?" He ignored my interruption and carried on with the most asinine briefing I ever attended. There were twice as many don'ts as there were do's and the only one that made any sense was… "If there are troops in contact with the enemy, forget the rules and do everything possible to render aid." I now see what Major Grady Morris was trying to tell us.

I won't try to list all the rules but one was: "If you sustain battle damage to your aircraft because you failed to heed the minimum altitude for pulling out of a dive on a bombing or strafing run, you could be court martialed." I wondered what would happen if you sustained battle damage AT minimum altitude. Would you only be half court martialed?

I must say that the briefing was one hellova a way to indoctrinate the new heads. I'd like to meet the weenie who dreamed up all of those asinine rules. I'll bet he never fired a shot in anger.

I already mentioned that I was impressed with the base facilities, but that was before I took a jeep tour of the entire

Base with Tom Normile and Charlie Rhymes. All of the enlisted men were living in tents in the most primitive conditions imaginable. I thought it was disgraceful and became determined to do something about it. Tom and Charlie agreed with me, which launched us on our scrounging spree.

After meeting with all of the aircraft commanders and GIBs, I could tell that all was not wine and roses in the ole 557th. Some guys came right out and voiced their complaints, while others just grumbled loud enough for me to hear them from a distance. Half of their problem was not having enough to do between missions… which was something I could fix.

The biggest complaint was directed at a small clique of aircraft commanders and GIBs who believed, because they'd been in-country the longest, they deserved preferential treatment when it came to scheduling missions up north. A hundred missions up north and you went home. I don't know how my predecessor handled the situation, but I suspected he had been a member of the clique, because he went home early.

I received the mission record of every aircrew member and there it was; a lopsided allotment of missions north that even a blind man could see. It was another thing I could fix. From then on I did the scheduling so everyone got their fair share of missions up north. One day one of the old heads approached me and demanded more missions north. So I made him the scheduling officer under my strict supervision. He then took his turns up north like the rest of us.

I became the sounding board of the squadron because of the way I handled the out of country missions. I didn't mind hearing people gripe as long as they did something to correct whatever it was that they were griping about. I didn't have any patience with those who griped just to be griping. It wasn't until I had every air crew gainfully employed with additional duty that the griping stopped… so I could get on with the war.

Although most of our missions were in South Vietnam, we did get more missions up north. Missions I was led to believe were commonplace back in the states.

My first few missions, beginning January 13th, were of the "tree busting" type. We would rendezvous with a Forward Air Controller (FAC) who was flying a twin engine OV-10, or a single engine Cessna O-2. His job was to spot supply dumps, truck parks, or troop concentrations in heavily wooded areas and mark the target with a white phosphorus rocket. If his rocket hit the target he would say, "Hit my smoke." If his rocket missed long, short, left or right of the target, he would call out so many clicks (meters) to compensate for the error.

Because of the heavy foliage, and the altitude that we were flying, we never saw what we were bombing. If we turned his white smoke black, the FAC was happy and we went home. Hence the name "tree busting" or "making tooth picks." We often got secondary explosions after a drop, which told us there had been something down there. It usually took a day or so before we would receive a Bomb Damage Assessment (BDA) from the FAC through Seventh Air Force.

We didn't always fly with the same GIB; the one I took a shine to was Lt. Dave Bump. He, like Tommy Almquist, was sharp as a tack and chomping at the bit to get in the front seat. I gave him as much stick time (flying from the back seat) as I got, including landing. He would have no problem upgrading to aircraft commander when he returned stateside.

Letters from home, along with goodie boxes, were the highlight of my day. Jeanne wrote two or three times a week keeping me abreast of things on the home front. A goodie box usually included homemade chocolate chip cookies. The BX at Cam Ranh Bay stocked everything imaginable, including cookies, but there's nothing that compares with homemade. I once wrote to tell Jeanne to double the amount of cookies being sent, because I always had a lot of 'friends' milling about whenever I opened a goodie box. But she went too far by addressing the next box to, Major Maultsby & Friends. I was away on a mission when the box arrived, so my 'Friends' opened it, helped themselves, and left only one cookie in the box on my desk.

Of the two hundred and sixteen missions I flew in Vietnam, only five were of any consequence as far as I was concerned. Even the seventy missions I flew in North Vietnam were of the hum-drum variety… except for one.

On 20 May, 1967, I was leading a flight of three on a typical tree busting mission just south of the DMZ (demilitarized zone). I received a call from an airborne command post directing me to divert and make haste to coordinates so and so. The coordinates put us forty miles north of the DMZ. They gave me a frequency to contact a

FAC who was in the area. It took just a few minutes to reach the area where the FAC was and make radio contact. He said a THUD (F-105) had been shot down along with an AIE that had attempted to suppress the flak so a chopper could get in to pick up the pilots. I had the FAC in sight and told him to pin point the area where the guns were located. He couldn't get close enough to fire a rocket, but instead tried to point out land marks leading to their positions. Making matters worse, I didn't know where the two downed pilots were. The FAC said he was in contact with the two pilots who were well hidden, but it was a matter of time before a ground party could reach them. We didn't have time.

I had a general idea where the guns were located, but couldn't know exactly where from an altitude of 12,000 feet. I told the other two aircraft to continue orbiting at 12,000 feet while I dropped down to have a look.

While passing through 5,000 feet, going like a bat out of hell, the 40 millimeters opened up from four different positions with Dave and me in the middle of the crossfire. It reminded me of Kunuri, Korea. I got tickled at Dave who would duck down behind the control panel every time a golf ball came close.

OK gang, now we know where they are so let's bounce a few 750s on them. While the other two aircraft rolled into their dive, I zoomed for altitude so I could join the party… not giving any thought to the 'rules of engagement.'
The flak became less intense after the other two aircraft made their passes. I couldn't tell if they had knocked out the guns because of all the thick smoke. But I could see another gun, very much alive, trying to zero in on Dave

and me. All the while I think the FAC was having an orgasm. Talk about an enthusiastic cheerleader! We were carrying six 750 pound bombs each plus a center line Gatling gun. I had briefed that we would drop two bombs each pass and use the gun to clear a path for the chopper if need be.

As I rolled in for my run, the other two aircraft were clawing for altitude, jinking all the way. As I positioned the pipper on the gun, I thought about what some Army troops had told me about finding dead gunners chained to their guns. These gunners were either chained, or very brave, because they didn't stop firing until the 750s straddled their position in a blinding flash.

Up till now none of us had noticed any small arms fire, but you never can tell. The FAC said neither downed pilot could detect fire other than the 40 millimeters. As I pulled out of the dive I could hear Dave grunt from the G force. Evidently we had silenced three of the four guns because we were only receiving fire from one position; or they were out of ammo. Three against one is never fair… unless your life is at stake.

The three of us made simultaneous runs from three different directions. Instead of concentrating on one of us, the gunner sprayed the area as if he'd gone berserk. The poor devil must have been chained to his gun and knew the jig was up. When the smoke cleared we could definitely confirm all the gun emplacements destroyed. You don't have to score a direct hit with a 750 pound bomb to wreak havoc. They're awesome.

Each of us had two bombs left, plus our Gatling guns, so

we hung around until the pilots were picked up by a Jolly Green (rescue chopper). I already made the decision to land at Da Nang to refuel because we didn't have enough to make it back to Cam Ranh.

We climbed up to 12,000 feet and orbited over the FAC while he directed the Jolly Green to the downed pilots. The pickup was successful with no other ground fire detected. We escorted the FAC and Jolly Green south of the DMZ and made a bee line to Da Nang. Not one of our aircraft received so much as a scratch.

Back at Cam Ranh there was the usual debriefing by Ops and intelligence; even the Information Officer was there. After giving a blow by blow account of our mission, the Awards and Decorations Officer announced that he was putting all of us in for a Distinguished Flying Cross (DFC). I already had two, but I was glad to see that Dave would get one. Sometime later, Dave and my DFCs were upgraded to Silver Stars by Seventh Air Force.

Most of the missions I flew north were at night. I preferred night missions because even small arms fire created a muzzle flash that could be seen for miles. Even a lighted match could be seen; a missile launch would certainly get your attention. The Ho Chi Minh trail was usually the target because of all the truck and other traffic headed south every night.

Most of the ACs and GIBS in the squadron didn't share my preference for night missions because they usually lasted two and a half to three hours, depending on the sector of the Ho Chi Minh trail's distance from Cam Ranh.

All missions require air to air refueling under blackout conditions. No lights of any kind on the tanker, or your aircraft, were illuminated. Rendezvous with the tanker was made using radar with a slow rate of closure. Even on the darkest night you could make out the tanker's outline from two or three hundred feet out. All refueling was done several miles out to sea to avoid ground fire.

We operated in elements of two aircraft; the number two aircraft trailing the leader by 1,000 feet. Once refueled, the lead aircraft would head for his sector of the Ho Chi Minh Trail dropping down to an altitude of between 5 to 6,000 feet, while his wingman would maintain 12,000 feet above and a mile astern. If the leader saw anything suspicious he would drop a flare and let his wingman unload on it with either his Gatling gun or 500 pound Hi Drag bombs. Very seldom did we receive ground fire before we unloaded on a suspect target. But afterwards… Wow!

Once the wingman's ammo was depleted, he would act as the flare ship and the leader would ride shotgun. There evidently were no radar controlled guns along the Ho Chi Minh Trail because all of the tracers I saw were usually a hundred yards behind the aircraft. They couldn't see us and likely fired at the sound of the aircraft. Radar controlled guns would have given us fits. If an element stopped a convoy, but ran out of ammo, it would call in another element to join the party.

The four squadrons of the 12th Tactical Fighter Wing took turns flying night missions monthly; one month night missions only, then three months day missions only.

A mission I looked forward to, but only flew six, was

escorting the Douglas EB-66s way up north where most of the action was. Their job was to sweep for enemy radar and jam it whenever there was to be a fighter or bomber sweep in the area. They were sitting ducks to the Migs, so it was our job to keep the Migs off of their backs.

A flight of four F-4Cs armed with air-to-air missiles (AIM-9 Sidewinder heat seeking missiles, and Aim-7 Sparrow radar guided missiles) would set up a trailing patrol slightly behind and 1,000 feet above the EB-66. An element of two F-4s would fly 500 to 1,000 feet left of the EB-66 while the other element flew right of the EB-66 at the same distance. Because the EB-66 was much slower than the F-4s, it was necessary for the elements to weave back and forth swapping positions. This also provided maximum visual coverage.

I was itching to get a Mig, but under no circumstances were we to leave the EB-66 unless it was attacked. I often saw Migs a mile or two in the distance, holding our heading and altitude, hoping we'd leave our escort job so their buddies could drop in from behind and claim a prize. Only once were SAMS (surface to air missiles) fired at us, but they didn't come close; the electronic warfare officers in the EB-66 were doing their jobs.

The most satisfying missions I flew while in Vietnam were those supporting the ground troops who were in contact with the enemy. Bombing a white puff of smoke in heavy foliage, and not seeing the results of your effort, was not my cup of tea. I liked to get down in the trenches with napalm and twenty mike mikes (20 millimeter), and on occasion, 500 pound high drags (500 pound bombs equipped with folding fins that extended when dropped, thus slowing the bomb down and allowing the aircraft an escape distance).

There were always two F-4s standing strip alert at the end of the runway, day and night, to support troops in contact. They were always configured with 20 mike mikes, 500 pound high drags, napalm and flares. Often only a few yards separated the friendlies from the bad guys.

I always sweated out having a 'Wing Weenie' attached to our squadron flying a mission with me. Whenever one would request a mission, I'd see to it that he was scheduled for a tree busting type. But you never knew when you might be diverted to support troops in contact where a 750 pound bomb was not the ordinance to use.

On several occasions, while leading a flight with a 'Wing Weenie' flying #4, I had to tell #4 to hold high and dry (remain at altitude and don't expend ordinance) if we were diverted to support troops. I don't mean to imply that all Wing personnel were less than proficient delivering ordinance, but one is too many.

A case in point: While flying in night weather, a Wing type became disoriented and lost control of his aircraft. He and his GIB punched out… and his GIB was killed. I felt responsible because I'd heard that the AC was incompetent. Fortunately I wasn't the one who had to refuse him more missions and he spent the duration behind a desk at Wing Headquarters.

Most close support missions I flew were without the benefit of a FAC. I'll never forget one mission that was almost comical had it not been serious business.

I was leading a flight of four on a tree busting mission with a full colonel flying #4. I knew the colonel couldn't hit his ass with both hands, but I didn't worry about it because one tree looked like another to him. As luck would have it, we were diverted to a fire base camp that was receiving mortar and rocket fire. The camp was located on a small hill where all trees and brush had been cleared for a hundred yards all around them to allow a clear field of fire. All fire base camps in South Vietnam were plotted on our maps with their call sign, radio frequency and co-ordinates. It only took us a few minutes to arrive over the camp and make contact.

The radio operator on the ground advised us that there was some confusion as to where the mortars were coming from, but they thought they were entrenched north of the camp. We circled the camp looking for a clearing where the mortars might be located; surely they couldn't fire a mortar through trees. The firing stopped when we approached the area.

I decided to saturate the area north of the camp when I saw one of our guys leap from the parapet on the northeast side of the camp and run like hell down the slope. When he reached the tree line, he hesitated for a split second, and then ran back up the hill as fast as he had run down the hill. A puff of white smoke arose out of the foliage. I couldn't believe my eyes! That little rascal had balls of brass and I made a mental note to try to meet him someday. Well, since he'd gone through all the trouble to mark the target, we'd just have to make it worth his effort.

I'd forgotten about #4 and his propensity to scatter bomb. The smoke grenade only let us know from which direction the mortars came, so we circled the hill in a clockwise direction starting at the tree line. We flew a loose echelon formation in order to get better coverage of the terrain below. We descended to 3,000 feet while straining to get a glimpse of a clearing.

We received a call from the camp that we were receiving light machine gun and small arms fire from the northeast sector; distance unknown. OK, let's arm em up, get some altitude, and do a little glide bombing.

Having no clue where the gunfire was emanating, I decided we'd saturate the area starting 100 yards northeast of the tree line and work our way out from the camp. #2 would drop a hundred yards out from my spot, and so on with #3, and #4. That should keep #4 well away from the camp.

Once we established four craters in a northeast direction, we would begin dropping a hundred yards long and short of our original drop.

Not wanting anyone to swing their nose through the camp with hot guns, we continued circling in a clockwise direction. Any fighter-bomber type knows you just didn't make multiple passes in the same direction without getting your fanny stitched. I just hoped my first two 750s would send the bad guys scrambling for cover and forget about shooting at us.

I warned the camp to keep their heads down as there may be a little hot shrapnel flying about. After my first drop the ground radio came up with, "Holy shit! If those bombs didn't kill 'em, they'll certainly be shell shocked!"

#2 and #3 did a good job of placing their bombs, but #4 pickled a little late and was about one hundred yards long. The bomb release button on the control stick grip is fondly called the pickle button. His next bomb was one hundred yards short, so he was back in the ball park. After three drops apiece, I figured we covered an area 200 X 300 yards.

All of this low altitude flying was gobbling up the fuel. But we weren't far from home plate, so I decided we would do a little low angle strafe. Not having a pin point target to aim at, we just sprayed the areas between the bomb craters. We managed to get in two strafe passes each before #4 called bingo fuel. The 200 X 300 yard area looked like the moon.

The camp thanked us for the firepower demonstration and said they would send a ground party out to see if we scored. One of many things I found repulsive about the war was the body count. The brass gauged the success of a mission, or campaign, by the number of bodies that were counted. God help us if, in the next war, we start collecting scalps. I'm getting too old to be a party in it.

Tom Normile, Charlie Rhymes and I, between missions, did what we could to improve living conditions among the enlisted personnel. Some things we did were legit and other things… not so legit. As I mentioned before, Cam Ranh was next to being stateside, with a well-equipped hospital, mess hall, BX, theater, and etc. It was also a port where most of the supplies from the States were off loaded.

The Officers Club on Cam Ranh was a favorite night spot

for Air Force, Army and civilian workers. It didn't take us long to befriend those who could do us a favor now and then… mostly now.

The number one priority was to get decent living quarters for the enlisted personnel. Quonset huts or trailers with air conditioning would do nicely. Tom Normile undertook this project working closely with a detachment of civilian engineers. Tom was Colonel Davis' aide which provided a subtle clout.

Charlie Rhymes and I found 42 TV sets in a warehouse that were just collecting dust. When we asked where the TVs were destined the answer was, "Probably the black market." I thought, no way! We borrowed an Army six-by, liberated the lot and stored them in a hangar. The ones not destined for the enlisted quarters would be good for bartering.

On June 19, 1967, Lt./Col. Adams completed his tour; Lt./Col. Fuller was made the squadron commander and I became his operations officer. By this time I had been in Vietnam a little more than six months. Lt./Col. Fuller suggested it was about time I went on R and R (rest and recuperation) for two weeks. I hadn't given the matter much thought because Seventh Air Force policy restricted anyone on R and R from going further east than Hawaii. Some fellas would have their wives meet them in Hawaii, but that was out of the question for Jeanne and me.

I'm not supposed to tell anyone… and everyone "knows" Americans didn't fly combat sorties in Cambodia… but somehow I led a flight of four into Cambodia well west of Saigon. A supply dump was the target we destroyed. We knew we wouldn't make it back to Cam Ranh, so we picked Bien Hoa Air Base, just north of Saigon, as a refueling stop. The U-2 outfit back at Davis-Monthan had an OL stationed at Bien Hoa where many of my old friends were.

While our aircraft were being serviced, I was invited to pass the time at the OL. During the course of our conversations, it was mentioned that a C-141 made a flight to Davis-Monthan and back every two weeks. The urge to see Jeanne and the boys was strong so I asked, "Do you think it would be possible for me to hitch a ride on the next flight to DM?" I was assured that it would not be a problem. All I had to do was say when. When I mentioned the travel restriction was that I go no further than Hawaii, the response was, "No sweat, we'll just cut the orders making you the courier." Hot damn, what a stroke of luck!

Back at Cam Ranh I told Tom and Charlie about my impending R and R. Charlie had already arranged to meet his wife in Hawaii, but Tom asked if he might go along because he hadn't been on R and R either. I suggested we both hop on a C-130 to Bien Hoa and ask.

The OL commander at Bien Hoa assured us that the C-141 could hold a whole bunch of people and it could be arranged for both Tom and me to act as couriers.

When the day arrived for Tom and me to board the C-141, the OL commander issued us a side arm and gave me an envelope. He explained that there was a one-of-a-kind camera in a crate on board and under no circumstances was it to be off loaded until the plane reached DM. If customs, or anyone else, tried to off load it, I was to show them the contents of the envelope.

All went well until we reached McChord AFB near Tacoma, Washington. There we were met by a brusque customs official who was determined to have us off load everything on board the aircraft, or else we wouldn't be allowed to take off.

When I handed him the envelope the OL commander had given me, he snatched it out of my hand and ripped it open. As he read the letter his face got as red as a beet. When he finished reading, he looked at Tom and me, then he looked at the 38 caliber pistols we were packing. Without a word he threw the letter down, spun on his heels and left.

Neither Tom nor I read the letter… until then. In essence, it said we were authorized to use whatever means necessary to prevent any downloading of the aircraft until it reached its final destination. If I had read the letter beforehand, I might have been tempted to shoot the bastard.

I hadn't notified Jeanne that I was on my way home to avoid any disappointment in case a glitch prevented my getting there. When I called her from Base Ops at Davis-Monthan she couldn't believe it. She knew about the travel restrictions for those in Vietnam and wondered how I pulled it off.

Jeanne and Kevin met Tom and me at Base Ops for one hellova reunion. Chuckie and Shawn were out and about somewhere when I called and couldn't be rounded up, but they would get a surprise later on. We dropped Tom off at the Tucson airport so he could get home. He'd call me later to find out when the C-141 would depart for Vietnam. The next week and a half went by so fast that there is little I remember other than the barrage of questions the boys asked about the war. Kevin, who was five at the time, kept insisting on seeing where I was wounded. He was sure that everyone who went to war got wounded... just like in the movies.

Tom arrived back in Tucson the day before the C-141 was scheduled to leave for the return flight, so he stayed the night with us for one last bash.

The first person Tom and I met when we arrived back at Cam Ranh was Col. Davis. He asked, "I haven't seen you two around for a couple of weeks, where have you been?" I answered, "We were on R and R sir." He then asked where we went. Tom and I were both thinking we were both in for it now when I answered, "We went home sir." "You went home!" Col. Davis exclaimed and then asked, "How the hell did you manage that?" After we told him the whole story he said, "Well I'll be damned!" He then asked, "Do you think you could set me up with a flight in the near future?" We assured him we could and with that, Col. Davis winked and left us standing there with our mouths open.

Some progress had been made on the enlisted men's quarters, but not enough to suit Tom. He rolled up his sleeves and became a man possessed. Meanwhile Charlie Rhymes met with a harrowing experience.

Charlie was flying a mission eighty miles north of the DMZ, when his aircraft was hit by ground fire. He immediately headed out to sea in case a bailout was in the cards. A mile off the coast his aircraft started burning and the flight controls became useless. The aircraft started porpoising. He tried to pull the ejection handles when he experienced positive Gs, but when the seat fired he was hanging on his seat belt. Charlie received compression fractures of the spine, but his GIB went unscathed. After they landed in the water, several small boats put off from shore, but the rest of his flight made short work of them with the Gatlings.

A Jolly Green soon had Charlie and his GIB in a hospital in Da Nang. He was later transferred to the hospital at Cam Ranh where Tom and I kept him supplied with medicinal martinis.

Charlie was released after his two week hospital stay and wasn't prepared for what he found when he entered his trailer… His mattress was rolled up neatly at the head of his bed. The sheets, blankets, and pillows were missing. His clothes, personal effects, toilet articles, and booze supply were gone. He was completely wiped out. Tom and I made sure we weren't around when he entered the trailer.

We gave Charlie twenty minutes to get over his initial shock before we showed up. His greeting was, "You dirty bastards, what did you do with my stuff?" I said, "Now Charlie, don't get your bowels in an uproar. When we heard that you had punched out we thought you had bought the farm. Tom and I were selected to survey your effects and ship them to your wife. She probably has them right now." With that, Charlie called us everything in the book but white men. It was all Tom and I could do to keep a straight face.

We let him rant and rave for a few more minutes before we burst out laughing and told him he could find all of his stuff in the trailer next door.

The VC (Viet Cong) never launched an attack on Cam Ranh during the ten months I was there. But my U-2 buddies at Bien Hoa caught hell on a regular basis. I had the misfortune of visiting them when the VC attacked with mortars and rockets one night inflicting heavy damage. The trailer I stayed in had several holes punched in it during the thirty minute barrage. Good thing I was in a bomb shelter at the time.

During that stay in Bien Hoa, a friend asked if I wanted to tag along on an errand to Seventh Air Force in Saigon. I said, "Sure, why not?" I wasn't one bit impressed with what I saw in Saigon and wished I hadn't come. All I saw were men and women racing around on motor scooters.

During our return to Bien Hoa, we were stopped to allow a column of American G.I.s cross the road. I got out of the jeep to talk to the sergeant who flagged us down. He told me the column had just gotten out of the field and were headed for a much needed rest. I stood there watching while about sixty G.I.s plodded along in single file. There was no joking or talking… nothing. They took no notice of me even though I was close enough to reach out and touch them. Their faces were drawn and haggard.

Their eyes stared vacantly at the man in front of them. Not one of them could have been more than twenty years old; some looked seventeen or eighteen. I thought about all the young Vietnamese men racing about on scooters in Saigon while our young men were doing their dirty work. I swore by God that Chuckie wouldn't be coming over here if I had to drive him to Canada myself! Chuckie would be draft age in several months.

I found out why Cam Ranh was never attacked by the VC while I was there from an Army officer I met in the Officers mess. He was an advisor attached to a ROK (Republic of Korea) unit whose mission was to guard Cam Ranh. I knew the ROK units were fierce fighters to the point of being ruthlessly sadistic. I learned this in Korea. What I learned about their guard tactics didn't make good dinner conversation.

Whenever the VC came close to striking distance with mortars and rockets, the ROKs would infiltrate their lines and capture a half dozen of them. Then the ROKs would return to their unit and skin their captives alive. They would place the bodies on poles placed about the perimeter of Cam Ranh, moving them further away each night until the VC got the hint and steered clear. Believe me, you can believe anything when it comes to the Koreans… North or South.

I can't conclude this chapter without mentioning the irony of all ironies. What follows is an additional endorsement, dated 27 October, 1967, Col. Woody Davis wrote on my efficiency report just before I left Vietnam:

I fully concur. I have observed this officer on a bi-weekly basis and feel this superior report is justly deserved. This officer is soft spoken, yet aggressive in the performance of his duties. There are no better strike or mission leaders in this Wing. This officer is dedicated to the role of tactical air power as attested to by his voluntary waiver of SEA assignment policies; as a previous prisoner of war he would not have been required to see action in SEA. I consider this a mark of a true professional. He has accomplished a great deal for the Wing and as a consequence should be promoted far ahead of his contemporaries

Now don't that beat all? I never volunteered for Vietnam, nor did I know about the policy not requiring ex-POWs to serve in SEA. Jeanne will have a shit-fit when she finds out. But what's done is done. But if I had known about that ex-POW policy, Jeanne and the boys would be in Germany right now.

Col. Davis, Col. McNeil and Lt./Col. Fuller had a meeting in Lt./Col. Fuller's office one afternoon when I received a call to join them. As I entered the office I immediately noticed the somber expressions on their faces and thought," Oh shit… what is it?" Col. Davis broke the ice with, "Chuck, you are setting a bad example around here. An officer with your experience should know by now how to wear a uniform." I suspected that he was pulling my leg, but it wasn't until he stood up and handed me a pair of silver leaves, that I knew for sure. Promotion to Lt./Col. hadn't entered my mind.

Well, the three of them had a good laugh and said they would meet me at the club for a celebration. I couldn't officially pin the silver leaves on until 20 December, 1967… I could wait.

I flew one more mission after reading Col. Davis' endorsement. It was a typical in-country, FAC directed, no sweat type mission.

I had been sitting alert when we were scrambled to an area northwest of Saigon. The FAC advised us that some VC were holed up in an abandoned church and asked us to light up a few candles. I thought it was an unlikely place for VC to hole up, but the FAC said some G.I.s were receiving fire from the church. He directed us to, "Make your run from east to west... some G.I.s are north of the church about two hundred yards. Two cans of napalm should do the job, but four would do it better."

The flat terrain was ideal for dropping napalm. We went in about fifty feet off the ground and scored direct hits. There was something other than VC in that church because the secondary explosions went off for at least ten minutes. The FAC reported that his little aircraft was buffeted by the shock waves. I informed the FAC we still had some high drags and twenty mike mikes, but he had no further use for them. I returned to base with 216 missions under my belt. But with no sense of accomplishment.

During debriefing the crew chief on the aircraft I just flew came in and said, "Major Maultsby, I thought you might like this little souvenir." He dropped a 30 caliber slug on the table and added, "I found it in the radome." The radome is the fiberglass housing on the nose of the aircraft where the radar is located. Some VC must have hit me a second before he was engulfed in napalm.

Tom Normile had written Col. Davis' endorsement on my efficiency report assuming I had volunteered for a tour in SEA. When he was informed otherwise, I was on my way home.

After an all-night bash in the Officers Club, I was hoisted aboard an airliner headed home on 4 November, 1967... and immediately fell asleep...

EPILOGUE

That tour of duty in Vietnam was no simple seventeen missions culminating in my being shot down. This time I survived an ordeal of two hundred and sixteen missions; seventy of them over North Vietnam where massively armed and skilled people on the ground, and in the air, were doing their best to kill me and my fellow pilots. They damn near succeeded.

I returned to the United States with a total of 233 combat missions (including the 17 in Korea), the Silver Star medal for Gallantry in Action, and the silver leaves of a Lieutenant Colonel on my shoulders.

A veteran war horse usually gets assigned a new job lacking the excitement of being attacked by Mig fighters, dodging the heaviest anti-aircraft fire in the world and the thrill of flying wildly to avoid the dogged pursuit of SAM missiles fired in volleys by angry Vietnamese.

There are those jobs, without the fury and roar of battle, that are often the most important. And my wife loved whatever the Air Force now wanted me to do… as long as I stayed put with the family in the States.

So… I became the Squadron Commander of the F-4 Replacement Training Unit with my new station at Davis-Monthan Air Force Base in Tucson, Arizona. It was grinding work giving orders, judging other pilots as I had once been judged and fighting new battles which included budget balancing and protocol. Oh!… and they promoted me to full bird colonel with the gleaming silver eagles on my shoulders... big deal.

Somehow, the chrome-domes in the Pentagon made their judgment that I should be raised steadily to jobs with greater importance; jobs with greater responsibility demanding of the kind of experience and skills I had collected. I wanted nothing more than to keep flying as my main occupation... but NO!

Colonel Maultsby was committed to a full tour in Headquarters of the Tactical Air Command.
Duty at TAC Headquarters is important as hell; no doubt about that. But I found myself leaving the war rooms and planning sessions to go outside and stare wistfully at the sky. But I did get to live in one of those beautiful English Tudor style homes that I had admired as a boy.

Then, finally, an overseas assignment! And this time Jeanne was going with me. Excitement raced through our lives again. The Air Force slated me for an assignment in Israel to work with that tightly knit and splendid air force. But I was never any good at speaking the Mongolian, Chinese or Hebrew languages. So it was laughable that my assignment was over before it started. I flunked the language aptitude test.

No loss, merely a sidestep to another overseas job that expanded the horizons and tastes of the Maultsby clan. I wound up in Naples, Italy for the next three years as the Chief of the Standardization and Evaluation Board for all Greek, Italian, Turkish and British fighter squadrons for NATO Forces South.

Good Lord! I'd become a high-ranking official! I had duties and responsibilities demanding smooth, but forceful relationships with our group speaking four languages, flying aircraft manufactured in a half-dozen different countries and always on the edge of knowing that, at any moment, we could be tangling with the Russian Bear.
I did it. I did a damn good job too… But this wasn't for me.

You start a kid out with a hop in a corrugated barnstormer taking off from a pasture. Add on the yellow-winged Cubs and their light weight brethren. Next, add the powerful piston jobs and fighters, and then add on the jet fighters. The kid experiences combat, surviving it all, then advancing to supersonic flight and floating like a long winged balloon over the top of the world… Then you chain him to a desk and… well… it's time to hang up the uniform. You can't ever regain that spark when you're a high official, and a high official was something I was never cut out to be.

So on July 1st of 1977, I retired. Not from flying, nor from life... I retired from stricture and uniform structure. I returned to the world within, where I had matured.

The kids weren't kids anymore and had their own lives to live. Jeanne and I bought a fifteen acre mini-ranch in the Texas hill country south of Austin. I fairly ran into this wonderful new life with the woman I loved so much who had either been at my side, or waiting for me to come home from tours and wars.

Out there in Texas I was still brimming over with the sensations of flight; and the wonders I had known in a lifetime nearly bursting with events, changes and growth. Jeanne and I became, what the locals described as, the "Pied Pipers of Valley View West." I had become history on the hoof. I became an elder statesman of flight.

I applied for, and attended a trade school in San Antonio, Texas. I rolled up the sleeves of my coveralls, in which I felt terrific, and dove into engines, airframes, parts and pieces of airplanes and whaddaya know. I became a licensed A&P mechanic (Airframe and Powerplant) with my license issued by the Federal Aviation Administration. I was as proud of that as any other certificate among the many that I'd tucked away in my wallet.

I was back flying as I had done so many decades before. The old fashioned flying, where you cruise low across the countryside enjoying the scenery, the smell of fresh rain, the smell of grease, gas and oil. Then back to the ground where I became spotted with grease and oil working on airplanes and imparting the lessons of flying and life to the youngsters who often flocked about me.

Then... there was one more important change after ten years in Texas.

I longed for the mountains and pines where summers have warm days and cool nights. I wanted to see winter snow falls and radiant changes of the seasons.

Colorado Springs, Colorado fit the bill, being on the edge of the Garden of the Gods in the Sangre de Christo Range of high mountains sweeping down to forested valleys. It's a different and wonderful world where even the sky is different.

There will always be the reminders of yesteryear; when a white contrail streaks the sky; when I see the silvery sweptwing reflections high above me in that bright and wonderful blue; when sounds ghost down to me from the heavens, a great bass viol whispering to me from the past from friends gone, but never forgotten.

I still look toward tomorrow. Tomorrow is the first day of something new, something different and who knows… perhaps something just as exciting as it will be unexpected.

Tomorrow is and will always be…

Toward the Unknown.

*   *   *

The Thunderbird Diamond Formation 1959

Top: Captain Chuck Maultsby (Right Wing)

Afterword...

Colonel Maultsby, my father, lost his final battle... to lung cancer and died in Tucson, Arizona on the morning of August 14th, 1998. He was 72 years old.

His lifelong love and devoted wife Jeanne, my mother, died on February 19th, 2012. She was 78 years old. She had missed him terribly.

Dad's friend, author Martin Caidin, was assisting him with editing his memoirs and would have been a great help in placing the book with a publisher. But Martin died about the time Dad's cancer became aggressive.

Mom and her sister, Betty, intended to finish the editing and publish Dad's story... but it was too difficult for her to deal with his passing and all the memories contained in his memoirs. It was my pleasure to honor my Father by finishing the process for us all... his is a story worthy of being told.

My brothers, Shawn and Kevin, are alive and well. Shawn lives in Colorado Springs, Colorado and Kevin lives in Reno, Nevada. My sons, Chuck E. and Stevie live in Tucson, Arizona.

My wife and I live near Arivaca, Arizona. I still sing with my band. My wife, Stacy, is a registered nurse. We met when she was Dad's hospice nurse during his last, extremely uncomfortable, months on earth. He had no doubt that she was heaven sent.

The following poem was Dad's favorite. It was inscribed on a brass plaque that hung in his home for as long as I can remember...

      Chuck W. Maultsby II
      February 9, 2013

"HIGH FLIGHT"

*Oh! I have slipped the surly bonds of Earth
And danced the skies on laughter-silvered wings;
Sunward I've climbed, and joined the tumbling mirth
Of sun-split clouds - and done a hundred things
You have not dreamed of - wheeled and soared and swung
High in the sunlit silence. Hov'ring there
I've chased the shouting wind along, and flung
My eager craft through footless halls of air...*

*Up, up the long, delirious, burning blue
I've topped the wind-swept heights with easy grace
Where never a lark or even eagle flew
And, while with silent, lifting mind I trod
The high untrespassed sanctity of space,
Put out my hand, and touched the face of God.*

    Pilot Officer John Gillespie Magee, Jr.

    #412 Squadron, RCAF...
    Killed 11 December 1941

Further reading related to, or featuring Col. Maultsby:

"Thunderbirds" and... *"The Silken Angels"* By... Martin Caidin

"We Rode the Thunder" By... The USAF Thunderbirds Alumni Association with Bob Gore

"Me and U-2: My Affair With The Dragon Lady" By... T/Sgt. Glenn R. Chapman United States Air Force (Retired)

"One Minute to Midnight: Kennedy, Khrushchev, and Castro on the Brink of Nuclear War" By... Michael Dobbs

"Remembering the Dragon Lady: Memoirs of the Men Who Experienced the Legend of the U-2 Spy Plane" By... Brig./Gen. Gerald McIlmoyle and Linda Rios Bromley

"Remembered Prisoners of a Forgotten War: An Oral History of Korean War Prisoners" By... Lewis H. Carlson

"In Enemy Hands: A Prisoner in North Korea" By...Larry Zellers

"Skunk Works: A Personal Memoir of My Years of Lockheed" By...Ben R. Rich and Leo Janos |

Made in the USA
Middletown, DE
20 July 2023